ARM 56 Course Guide

Risk Financing
6th Edition

The Institutes
720 Providence Road, Suite 100
Malvern, Pennsylvania 19355-3433

6th Edition • 2nd Printing • May 2015

ISBN 978-0-89463-621-9

Contents

Study Materials iii

Student Resources iv

Using This Course Guide iv

Assignments

1. Introduction to Risk Financing 1.1

2. Estimating Hazard Risk 2.1

3. Transferring Hazard Risk Through Insurance 3.1

4. Self-Insurance Plans 4.1

5. Retrospective Rating Plans 5.1

6. Reinsurance 6.1

7. Captive Insurance 7.1

8. Contractual Risk Transfer 8.1

9. Transferring Financial Risk 9.1

10. Transferring Hazard Risk to the Capital Markets 10.1

11. Allocating Costs of Managing Hazard Risk 11.1

Exam Information 1

 ## Study Materials Available for ARM 56

Risk Financing, 6th ed., 2012, AICPCU.

ARM 56 *Course Guide*, 6th ed., 2012, AICPCU (includes access code for SMART Online Practice Exams).

ARM 56 SMART Study Aids—Review Notes and Flash Cards, 6th ed.

Student Resources

Catalog A complete listing of our offerings can be found in The Institutes' professional development catalog, including information about:

- Current programs and courses
- Current textbooks, course guides, SMART Study Aids, and online offerings
- Program completion requirements
- Exam registration

To obtain a copy of the catalog, visit our website at www.TheInstitutes.org or contact Customer Service at (800) 644-2101.

How to Prepare for Institutes Exams This free handbook is designed to help you by:

- Giving you ideas on how to use textbooks and course guides as effective learning tools
- Providing steps for answering exam questions effectively
- Recommending exam-day strategies

The handbook is printable from the Student Services Center on The Institutes' website at www.TheInstitutes.org or available by calling Customer Service at (800) 644-2101.

Educational Counseling Services To ensure that you take courses matching both your needs and your skills, you can obtain free counseling from The Institutes by:

- Emailing your questions to Advising@TheInstitutes.org
- Calling an Institutes' counselor directly at (610) 644-2100, ext. 7601
- Obtaining and completing a self-inventory form, available on our website at www.TheInstitutes.org or by contacting Customer Service at (800) 644-2101

Exam Registration Information As you proceed with your studies, be sure to arrange for your exam.

- Visit our website at www.TheInstitutes.org/forms to access and print the Registration Booklet, which contains information and forms needed to register for your exam.
- Plan to register with The Institutes well in advance of your exam.

How to Contact The Institutes For more information on any of these publications and services:

- Visit our website at www.TheInstitutes.org
- Call us at (800) 644-2101 or (610) 644-2100 outside the U.S.
- Email us at CustomerService@TheInstitutes.org
- Fax us at (610) 640-9576
- Write to us at The Institutes, Customer Service, 720 Providence Road, Suite 100, Malvern, PA 19355-3433

Using This Course Guide

This course guide will help you learn the course content and prepare for the exam.

Each assignment in this course guide typically includes the following components:

Educational Objectives These are the most important study tools in the course guide. Because all of the questions on the exam are based on the Educational Objectives, the best way to study for the exam is to focus on these objectives.

Each Educational Objective typically begins with one of the following action words, which indicate the level of understanding required for the exam:

Analyze—Determine the nature and the relationship of the parts.

Apply—Put to use for a practical purpose.

Associate—Bring together into relationship.

Calculate—Determine numeric values by mathematical process.

Classify—Arrange or organize according to class or category.

Compare—Show similarities and differences.

Contrast—Show only differences.

Define—Give a clear, concise meaning.

Describe—Represent or give an account.

Determine—Settle or decide.

Evaluate—Determine the value or merit.

Explain—Relate the importance or application.

Identify or list—Name or make a list.

Illustrate—Give an example.

Justify—Show to be right or reasonable.

Paraphrase—Restate in your own words.

Recommend—Suggest or endorse something to be used.

Summarize—Concisely state the main points.

Outline The outline lists the topics in the assignment. Read the outline before the required reading to become familiar with the assignment content and the relationships of topics.

Key Words and Phrases These words and phrases are fundamental to understanding the assignment and have a common meaning for those working in insurance. After completing the required reading, test your understanding of the assignment's Key Words and Phrases by writing their definitions.

Review Questions The review questions test your understanding of what you have read. Review the Educational Objectives and required reading, then answer the questions to the best of your ability. When you are finished, check the answers at the end of the assignment to evaluate your comprehension.

Application Questions These questions continue to test your knowledge of the required reading by applying what you've studied to "hypothetical" real-life situations. Again, check the suggested answers at the end of the assignment to review your progress.

Sample Exam Your course guide includes a sample exam (located at the back) or a code for accessing SMART Online Practice Exams (which appears on the inside of the cover). Use the option available for the course you're taking to become familiar with the test format.

For courses that offer SMART Online Practice Exams, you can either download and print a sample credentialing exam or take full practice exams using questions like those that will appear on your credentialing exam. SMART Online Practice Exams are as close as you can get to experiencing an actual exam before taking one.

More Study Aids

The Institutes also produce supplemental study tools, called SMART Study Aids, for many of our courses. When SMART Study Aids are available for a course, they are listed on page iii of the course guide. SMART Study Aids include Review Notes and Flash Cards and are excellent tools to help you learn and retain the information in each assignment.

A

Assignment 1
Introduction to Risk Financing

Assignment 2
Estimating Hazard Risk

Assignment 3
Transferring Hazard Risk Through Insurance

Assignment 4
Self-Insurance Plans

Direct Your Learning ▶▶

Introduction to Risk Financing

Educational Objectives

After learning the content of this assignment, you should be able to:

1. Describe risk financing and its importance to organizations.

2. Describe common risk financing goals for organizations.

3. Explain how to evaluate a risk in order to select a risk financing plan.

4. Explain how enterprise risk management (ERM) takes a holistic approach to managing risk.

Outline

▶ **Introduction to Risk Financing**
  A. Risk Financing as a Part of Risk Treatment
  B. Risk Transfer
     1. Insurance
     2. Contract (Noninsurance)
     3. Hedging
  C. Risk Retention
     1. Planned or Unplanned
     2. Complete or Partial
     3. Funded or Unfunded

▶ **Risk Financing Goals**
  A. Pay for Negative Financial Consequences of an Event
  B. Maintain Liquidity
  C. Manage Uncertainty
  D. Comply With Legal and Regulatory Requirements
  E. Minimize the Cost of Risk
     1. Administrative Expenses
     2. Loss Control Expenses
     3. Retained Losses
     4. Transfer Costs

▶ **Selecting a Risk Financing Plan**
  A. Hazard Risk
     1. Frequency and Severity Characteristics of Hazard Losses
     2. The Prouty Approach
     3. Relationship Between Characteristics of Hazard Losses and Risk Financing Plans
     4. Categories of Hazard Risk Financing Plans
  B. Financial Risk

▶ **Managing Risk Holistically**
  A. Categories of Risk
  B. ERM Versus Traditional Risk Management
  C. Managing Risks as a Whole

s.m.a.r.t.®
tips

Don't spend time on material you have already mastered. The SMART Review Notes are organized by the Educational Objectives found in each assignment to help you track your study.

For each assignment, you should define or describe each of the Key Words and Phrases and answer each of the Review and Application Questions.

Educational Objective 1
Describe risk financing and its importance to organizations.

Key Words and Phrases

Risk financing

Transfer

Retention

Hazard risk

Speculative risk

Insurance

Risk

Hold-harmless agreement (or indemnity agreement)

Hedging

Futures contract

Review Questions

1-1. Describe the two categories of risk financing techniques.

1-2. Describe what risk transfer shifts to another party through insurance and noninsurance techniques.

1-3. Explain when hedging is practical.

Application Question

1-4. John is a risk management professional for his employer. His employer's management is trying to decide whether to retain some of the financial consequences of general liability events or transfer them to an insurer. What advantages of transferring the financial consequences of general liability events to an insurer might John point out to management?

Educational Objective 2
Describe common risk financing goals for organizations.

Key Words and Phrases

Liquid asset

Risk management framework

Review Questions

2-1. Describe an organization's sources of liquidity.

2-2. Describe the standards set by the Sarbanes–Oxley Act of 2002.

2-3. Name the primary measure used by many organizations to gauge the effectiveness of their insurance risk management program.

Application Question

2-4. Michelle is a risk management professional for a pharmaceutical manufacturer. The company's management is considering retaining a large portion of its products liability losses. What factors could Michelle bring to management's attention to support retaining such losses?

Educational Objective 3
Explain how to evaluate a risk in order to select a risk financing plan.

Key Words and Phrases

Risk criteria

Hard market

Soft market

Review Questions

3-1. Describe what the frequency of losses is.

3-2. Describe what the severity of a loss is.

3-3. Explain how the broad categories of the Prouty Approach are still useful despite being subjective.

3-4. Describe risk financing hybrid plans.

Application Question

3-5. Maggie is the risk management professional for a large manufacturer. The company's management has taken an aggressive approach to risk, in Maggie's opinion. Management assumes its large size will allow it to retain more risk than Maggie believes is appropriate. What should Maggie point out to her management?

Educational Objective 4
Explain how enterprise risk management (ERM) takes a holistic approach to managing risk.

Key Words and Phrases

Enterprise risk management

Business risk

Review Questions

4-1. Explain why an organization may decide to manage its business risks using an enterprise risk management (ERM) approach.

4-2. Identify the ERM categories of risk.

4-3. Describe the differences between enterprise risk management and traditional risk management.

Answers to Assignment 1 Questions

NOTE: These answers are provided to give students a basic understanding of acceptable types of responses. They often are not the only valid answers and are not intended to provide an exhaustive response to the questions.

Educational Objective 1

1-1. Risk financing techniques can be categorized as either risk transfer or risk retention.

1-2. Risk transfer shifts the financial consequences of an event to another party through insurance and noninsurance techniques.

1-3. Hedging is practical when it is used to offset the consequences of risk to which one is naturally, voluntarily, or inevitably exposed.

1-4. John could explain to management that they would be substituting a small certain financial cost, the insurance premium, for the possibility of a large uncertain financial loss, paid by the insurer. Insurance is essentially a funded risk transfer. By accepting a premium, the insurer agrees to pay for all of the organization's losses that are covered by the insurance contract. The insurer also agrees to provide services, such as claims handling and defense of liability claims.

Educational Objective 2

2-1. An organization's sources of liquidity include the liquidity of its assets, the strength of its cash flows, its borrowing capacity, and (for a publicly traded organization) its ability to issue stock.

2-2. Sarbanes–Oxley sets new or more stringent standards for all U.S. public company boards. Such standards include requirements that senior executives take personal responsibility for the accuracy and completeness of corporate financial reports by certifying and approving the integrity of their reports quarterly. Sarbanes–Oxley also modifies reporting requirements for financial transactions, including off-balance sheet transactions, pro-forma figures, stock transactions of corporate officers, and timely notice of material changes in financial condition.

2-3. Managing the cost of risk is the primary measure used by many organizations to gauge the effectiveness of their insurance risk management program.

2-4. Michelle could point out that the company should compare the projected cost of retaining such losses with the cost of transferring them. Product liability claims from drugs could develop years after the drugs are sold and consumed. That would cause significant delays in claim reporting and settlement offers. Such losses are often referred to as long-tail losses. Long-tail losses are not paid to claimants immediately but instead are paid over time. Therefore, the company can invest those amounts until losses are paid.

Michelle should measure the value of such deferred loss payments when analyzing the cost of the company's loss retention program. Deferring loss payments lowers the company's cost of risk.

She could also point out when deciding whether to retain or transfer the company's losses that the company should take into account the value of the cash flow benefit from retaining losses. A premium paid to an insurer to transfer losses is usually due at the beginning of the policy period, whereas retained losses are paid at later dates, generating a cash flow benefit to the company and, therefore, lowering its present value costs.

Educational Objective 3

3-1. The frequency of losses is the number of losses that occur within a specified period.

3-2. The severity of a loss is the amount of a loss, typically measured in monetary units, such as dollars.

3-3. Although the broad categories of loss frequency and loss severity of the Prouty Approach are subjective, they provide risk management professionals with a means of justifying the priority that they believe should be placed on the various risks confronting the organization and a means of providing risk treatment suggestions.

3-4. Risk financing hybrid plans combine retention and transfer, so they can apply to all losses, regardless of their severity. Hybrid plans combine the elements of both loss retention and loss transfer. For example, a large-deductible insurance plan can be designed to cover all losses that an organization incurs by retaining losses up to the large deductible amount and transferring losses beyond that amount.

3-5. Maggie can explain that the risk criteria management has set as her benchmark are inaccurate for the company's level of risk. The level of risk is a relative measure of the likelihood or frequency of losses combined with the consequences or severity of the company's aggregate losses. The higher the level of risk, the less likely the company would choose to retain losses and the more likely it is to transfer them or at least choose a hybrid combination of retention and transfer.

Educational Objective 4

4-1. An organization may decide to manage its business risks by using an ERM approach to maximize shareholder value.

4-2. ERM classifies risk into four categories:

- Strategic risks—uncertainties associated with the organization's overall long-term goals and management

- Operational risks—uncertainties associated with the organization's operations

- Financial risks—uncertainties associated with the organization's financial activities

- Hazard risks—uncertainties associated with the organization's reduction in value resulting from the effects of accidental losses

4-3. ERM differs from traditional risk management in key ways:

- ERM encompasses both hazard risk and business risk; traditional risk management focuses on hazard risk.

- ERM seeks to enable an organization to fulfill its greatest productive potential; traditional risk management seeks to restore an organization to its former pre-loss condition.

- ERM focuses on the value of the organization; traditional risk management focuses on the value of the accidental loss.

- ERM focuses on the organization as a whole; therefore, traditional risk management is both its own discipline and part of the broader enterprise risk management discipline.

Direct Your Learning

2

Estimating Hazard Risk

After learning the content of this assignment, you should be able to:

1. Explain how to analyze and evaluate hazard risk.
2. Explain how to estimate expected losses arising from hazard risk.
3. Explain how to apply increased limit factors to hazard loss estimates.
4. Explain how to estimate the volatility of hazard losses.

Outline

▶ **Analyzing and Evaluating Hazard Risk**

   A. Quantitative Versus Qualitative Analysis

   B. Hazard Risk Evaluation

▶ **Steps in Estimating Hazard Losses**

   A. Overview of the Procedure

   B. Step 1: Collect and Organize Past Data

      1. Loss Data

      2. Exposure Data

   C. Step 2: Limit Individual Losses

   D. Step 3: Apply Trend and Loss Development Factors to the Data

      1. Loss Development

      2. Loss Development Factors

      3. Calculating Loss Development Factors

      4. Trend Factors

   E. Step 4: Forecast Losses

▶ **Applying Increased Limit Factors**

   A. Overview of the Procedure

   B. Step One—Developing Increased Limit Factors

   C. Step Two—Calculating the Increased Limit Factor for a Specific Layer of Losses

   D. Step Three—Forecasting Losses at Various Loss Limits

▶ **Estimating Hazard Loss Volatility**

   A. Forecasting Probable Variation From Expected Loss

      1. Frequency Probability Distribution

      2. Severity Probability Distribution

      3. Total Loss Probability Distribution

   B. Probability Intervals

s.m.a.r.t. tips   Reduce the number of Key Words and Phrases that you must review. SMART Flash Cards contain the Key Words and Phrases and their definitions, allowing you to set aside those cards that you have mastered.

▶▶

For each assignment, you should define or describe each of the Key Words and Phrases and answer each of the Review and Application Questions.

Educational Objective 1
Explain how to analyze and evaluate hazard risk.

Key Words and Phrases

Pure risk

Law of large numbers

Review Questions

1-1. Explain what is assumed in quantitative analysis when analyzing the data of past losses.

1-2. Describe what estimating losses qualitatively draws upon from practitioners in relevant fields.

1-3. Explain how the level of risk can be used in budgeting.

1-4. Describe the diversification benefit of hazard risk.

Application Question

1-5. Bob is a risk management professional for a restaurant that has one location. The restaurant has been in continuous operation for ten years. Bob's boss wants to know whether the organization can use its own past losses to predict two types of losses in the future. The first type of loss is from customers leaving the restaurant without paying their entire bill, which has a high frequency but low severity. The second type is kitchen fire, which has low frequency but high severity.

Educational Objective 2
Explain how to estimate expected losses arising from hazard risk.

Key Words and Phrases

Paid losses

Loss reserve

Loss adjustment expense reserves

Incurred losses

Loss development

Loss payout pattern

Exposure unit

Increased limit factor table

Trend factor

Loss development factor

Ultimate loss development factor

Loss triangle

Review Questions

2-1. Identify the four steps a risk management professional should complete to prepare an estimate of hazard losses.

2-2. Identify the past loss data required to determine incurred losses.

2-3. Explain why risk management professionals limit losses.

2-4. Explain why the ultimate loss development factors bear an inverse relationship to the age of each accident year.

2-5. Explain why an organization's estimated ultimate incurred losses and exposure base data must be adjusted for inflation to the forecasted year.

Application Question

2-6. Listed below are the amounts paid to date and the current loss reserves for six liability claims incurred in 20X0 and evaluated as of 6/30/20X1, eighteen months after the beginning of the calendar year 20X0.

20X0 Claim	Claim Evaluation as of 6/20/20X1		Incurred Losses
	Paid Losses	Loss Reserves	
A	$46,000	$90,000	$
B	$10,000	$0	$
C	$15,000	$11,000	$
D	$4,000	$1,000	$
E	$87,000	$50,000	$
F	$14,000	$30,000	$
Totals			

The following questions relate to the claims listed in this table.

a. What is the total estimated value of incurred losses for the six claims as of the 6/30/20X1 evaluation date?

b. Calculate the estimated value of incurred claims if each claim is limited to < $20,000 and < $50,000:

Educational Objective 3
Explain how to apply increased limit factors to hazard loss estimates.

Key Word or Phrase

Increased limit factor

Review Questions

3-1. Explain why insurance advisory organizations develop increased limit factors from aggregated insurer data.

3-2. Explain how the average expected losses for an upper layer of limits is determined after the total average expected losses for all layers has been calculated.

▶▶

3-3. Explain how an organization can use the knowledge of the total average expected losses up to a $1 million limit.

Application Question

3-4. Cindy owns and operates a fine restaurant. Enough of her own past general liability losses are limited to $25,000 to be statistically credible. She has estimated such losses will total $200,000 next year. She has had a few larger losses and knows more could occur. Industry-wide data are not available, but increased limit factor tables are. Cindy wants to know what the average expected general liability losses are in the $25,000 to $500,000 layer. The increased limit factor for the loss limit of $500,000 is 2.70. The same factor for the loss limit of $25,000 is 1.20.

a. Calculate the increased limit factor from $25,000 to $500,000.

b. Calculate the expected losses at the $500,000 limit.

   c. Calculate the average expected general liability losses in the $25,000 to $500,000 layer.

Educational Objective 4
Explain how to estimate the volatility of hazard losses.

Key Words and Phrases

Frequency probability distribution

Severity probability distribution

Total loss probability distribution

Expected value

Review Questions

4-1. Identify the three types of probability distributions used to estimate the probability of alternate total loss outcomes.

4-2. Explain how the expected value of the losses of an organization's frequency distribution is determined.

4-3. Explain what it means when a positively skewed curve is superimposed over an organization's frequency probability distribution.

4-4. Explain how the mean or average severity of an organization's losses in a severity probability distribution can be determined.

4-5.   Describe what a probability interval represents.

Application Questions

4-6.   Use the following data from an organization to calculate the total mean severity:

	Severity Range	Mean Severity	Probability	Mean Severity × Probability
A	$5,000–$9,999	$	0.40	$
B	$10,000–$14,999	$	0.30	$
C	$15,000–$19,999	$	0.20	$
D	$20,000–$24,999	$	0.07	$
E	$25,000 and over	$	0.03	$
	Total		1.00	$

4-7.   Using probability intervals, if the total losses for an oganizaation fall between $10,000 and $20,000 in five out of ten years, the five years constitute a probability interval of what percent?

Answers to Assignment 2 Questions

NOTE: These answers are provided to give students a basic understanding of acceptable types of responses. They often are not the only valid answers and are not intended to provide an exhaustive response to the questions.

Educational Objective 1

1-1. It is assumed when analyzing the data of past losses that what occurred in the past will occur in the future.

1-2. Estimating losses qualitatively draws upon the education, training, and expertise of practitioners in relevant fields to estimate, in their judgment, the probabilities that certain losses will occur.

1-3. An organization will usually want to include in its budget a sufficient amount to pay the portion of expected losses that it plans to retain.

1-4. Hazard risk is generally not correlated with the organization's other types of risks, such as operational, financial, and strategic risks, which provides a diversification benefit. When a hazard risk loss occurs, it does not usually increase the likelihood or negative consequences of events from other types of risk.

1-5. Because the restaurant has been in continuous operation for ten years, Bob should have enough internal losses that have high frequency and low severity, such as the first type of losses (customers leaving without paying their entire bill), to estimate with reasonable creditability the future amount of these losses. However, the restaurant has a lack of operational diversification since it operates in only one location. Lack of diversification may prevent Bob from estimating with the same reasonable credibility the future amount of the second type of losses (kitchen fires) that have low frequency and high severity.

Educational Objective 2

2-1. Estimating hazard losses (dollar amounts) entails calculating an estimate of the expected (or average) losses for the coming year based on past data, which requires an organization's risk management professional to complete these four steps:

- Collect and organize past data

- Limit individual losses

- Apply trend and loss development factors to the data

- Forecast losses

2-2. Past loss data required to determine incurred losses include paid losses, loss reserves, and loss adjustment expense reserves.

2-3. Risk management professionals limit losses to match the range of losses or layers being forecast. Limiting losses stabilizes them. That is, an organization's losses do not vary significantly from year to year when losses that exceed a certain level are capped. This allows a risk management professional to focus on the layer of losses that have sufficient frequency to be predictable and, therefore, retainable.

2-4. The ultimate loss development factors applied bear an inverse relationship to the age of each accident year because most loss development occurs early in the life of a claim.

2-5. An organization's estimated ultimate incurred losses and exposure base data must be adjusted for inflation to the forecasted year to make the data comparable.

2-6.

a. The total estimated value of incurred claims as of the 6/30/20X1 evaluation date equals the total of paid losses and loss reserves for each claim ($358,000), calculated as follows:

Claim Evaluation as of 6/20/20X1			
20X0 Claim	Paid Losses	Loss Reserves	Incurred Losses
A	$ 46,000	$ 90,000	$ 136,000
B	$ 10,000	$ 0	$ 10,000
C	$ 15,000	$ 11,000	$ 26,000
D	$ 4,000	$ 1,000	$ 5,000
E	$ 87,000	$ 50,000	$ 137,000
F	$ 14,000	$ 30,000	$ 44,000
Totals	$176,000	$182,000	$ 358,000

b. These are the estimated values of incurred claims if each claim is limited to < $20,000:

- A $20,000
- B 10,000
- C 20,000
- D 5,000
- E 20,000
- F 20,000

Total: $95,000

These are the estimated values of incurred claims if each claim is limited to < $50,000:

- A $50,000
- B 10,000
- C 26,000
- D 5,000
- E 50,000
- F 44,000

Total: $185,000

Educational Objective 3

3-1. Insurance advisory organizations develop increased limit factors from aggregated insurer data because few insurers would have sufficient claims in high-limit layers to make conclusive loss forecasts.

3-2. The average expected losses for an upper layer of limits is determined by subtracting the expected losses of the lower layers from the average expected losses for all layers.

3-3. An organization can use this knowledge in at least two ways. First, it may want to assess whether it can comfortably afford to retain losses up to the amount of the total average expected losses. If so, it may want to consider raising its deductible up to the high limit. Second, the organization may want to assess whether the premium charged by its insurer for $1 million of coverage is reasonable when considering the amount of the total average expected losses.

3-4. These answers pertain to questions about Cindy's case:

   a. Using the increased limit factor for the loss limit of $500,000 of 2.70 and 1.20 for the loss limit of $25,000, the increased limit factor from $25,000 to $500,000 can be calculated by dividing 2.70 by 1.20. The result is 2.25.

   b. The losses at the $500,000 limit can be calculated by multiplying the increased limit factor from $25,000 to $500,000 of 2.25 by the estimated losses under $25,000, which is $200,000. The result is $450,000.

   c. The average expected general liability losses in the $25,000 to $500,000 layer can be determined by subtracting the expected losses under $25,000 of $200,000 from the expected losses at the $500,000 limit of $450,000. The result is $250,000.

Educational Objective 4

4-1. To estimate the probability of alternative total loss outcomes, three types of probability distributions are analyzed:

- Frequency probability distribution
- Severity probability distribution
- Total loss probability distribution

4-2. The expected value of the losses of an organization's frequency distribution is determined by multiplying each possible outcome by its probability and summing the results.

4-3. A positively skewed curve that is superimposed over a frequency probability distribution of an organization indicates loss frequencies are concentrated at low-frequency levels to the left of the curve. Further, as severity increases, frequency decreases.

4-4. The mean or average severity of an organization's losses in a severity probability distribution can be determined by multiplying the average severity outcome in each range by the probability of the losses falling within that range.

4-5. A probability interval is a representation that shows the probability of outcomes falling within certain ranges of a probability distribution.

4-6. The mean severity is calculated as follows:

Severity Range	Mean Severity	Probability	Mean Severity × Probability
$5,000–$9,999	$ 7,500	0.40	$ 3,000
$10,000–$14,999	$12,500	0.30	$ 3,750
$15,000–$19,999	$17,500	0.20	$ 3,500
$20,000–$24,999	$22,500	0.07	$ 1,575
$25,000 and over	$25,000	0.03	$ 750
Total		1.00	$12,575

4-7. The five years constitute a probability interval of 50 percent.

Direct Your Learning

Transferring Hazard Risk Through Insurance

Educational Objectives

After learning the content of this assignment, you should be able to:

1. Describe the purpose and operation of insurance, including risk reduction through pooling and services provided by insurers.

2. Explain how insurance benefits individuals, organizations, and society.

3. Describe the characteristics of an ideally insurable loss exposure.

4. Describe the types of property and liability deductibles.

5. Describe the purpose, operation, advantages, and disadvantages of large deductible plans.

6. Explain why organizations need excess and/or umbrella liability insurance.

7. Describe the basic differences between excess liability insurance and umbrella liability insurance.

8. Describe the different types of excess liability insurance and how each operates.

9. Explain how excess and umbrella liability insurance can be used in a layered liability insurance program, and describe the problems that may occur.

10. Describe the options for structuring an international insurance program.

Outline

▶ **Purpose and Operation of Insurance**

  A. Pooling

    1. How Pooling Reduces Risk

    2. How the Law of Large Numbers Explains Pooling

    3. How Positively Correlated Losses Affect a Pool

    4. How Insurance Differs From Pooling

  B. Insurer-Provided Risk Management Services

    1. Risk Control Services

    2. Claim and Legal Services

▶ **Benefits of Insurance**

  A. Paying for Losses

  B. Managing Cash Flow Uncertainty

  C. Meeting Legal Requirements

  D. Promoting Risk Control

  E. Enabling Efficient Use of Resources

  F. Providing Support for Insured's Credit

  G. Providing Source of Investment Funds

  H. Reducing Social Burdens

▶ **Ideally Insurable Loss Exposures**

  A. Pure Risk

  B. Accidental Loss

  C. Definite in Time and Measurable

  D. Large Number of Similar, Independent Exposures

  E. Not Simultaneous and Not Catastrophic

  F. Economically Feasible to Insure

▶ **Deductibles**

    1. Property Deductibles

    2. Liability Deductibles

▶ **Large Deductible Plans**

  A. Purpose and Operation of Large Deductible Plans

    1. Large Deductible Versus Self-Insured Retention (SIR)

    2. Uses of Large Deductible Plans

  B. Advantages and Disadvantages of Large Deductible Plans

▶ **Need for Excess or Umbrella Liability Coverage**

  A. Difficulty in Estimating Maximum Possible Loss

  B. Layering of Liability Coverages

  C. Effect of Aggregate Limits

▶ **Basic Differences: Excess and Umbrella Liability Policies**

▶ **Excess Liability Insurance**

  A. Following-Form Excess Liability Policies

  B. Self-Contained Excess Liability Policies

  C. Combination Excess Liability Policies

  D. Specific and Aggregate Excess Liability Insurance

▶ **Structuring a Liability Insurance Program**

  A. Working Layer and Buffer Layer

  B. Problems in Layering Coverage

  C. Adequacy of Excess Liability Limits

▶ **Structuring an International Insurance Program**

  A. Admitted Versus Nonadmitted Insurance

  B. Exporters Package Policy

  C. Controlled Master Program

    1. Advantages of Controlled Master Programs

    2. Disadvantages of Controlled Master Programs

s.m.a.r.t.® tips   Actively capture information by using the open space in the SMART Review Notes to write out key concepts. Putting information into your own words is an effective way to push that information into your memory.

For each assignment, you should define or describe each of the Key Words and Phrases and answer each of the Review and Application Questions.

Educational Objective 1

Describe the purpose and operation of insurance, including risk reduction through pooling and services provided by insurers.

Key Words and Phrases

Pool

Risk charge

Counterparty risk

Review Questions

1-1. Identify the circumstances under which pooling reduces risk.

1-2. Describe the effect of pooling on an organization's expected accidental losses.

1-3. Describe the typical distribution of positively correlated losses.

1-4. Contrast insurance and pooling.

1-5. Describe the services, in addition to risk transfer, that are often provided by insurers.

Application Question

1-6. The Kendall Bus Company is a publicly held corporation providing school bus transportation to public and private schools in Midland County. Kendall owns 200 school buses, located in three different cities within the county. Its major competitors are two larger bus companies that operate in the same general area.

a. Of the exposures Kendall faces, give an example of a correlated loss exposure and an uncorrelated loss exposure. (Answers may vary.)

b. Suppose Kendall were to enter into a formal arrangement with the Green Bus Company, a similar company that operates in another state, to pool the losses suffered by both companies. How would this affect Kendall's risks with respect to the two loss exposures previously identified? Explain your answer.

c. Suppose, instead, Kendall were to participate in a formal pool with fifteen other school bus companies. How, if at all, would this affect Kendall's risks with respect to each of the previously identified loss exposures? Explain.

Educational Objective 2

Explain how insurance benefits individuals, organizations, and society.

Review Questions

2-1. List the ways insurance benefits individuals, organizations, and society.

2-2. Explain how an organization can achieve risk financing goals through the use of insurance.

2-3. List risk-sharing mechanisms an insurer may use to promote risk control.

Educational Objective 3
Describe the characteristics of an ideally insurable loss exposure.

Review Questions

3-1. Insurers generally prefer to provide insurance for loss exposures that have certain characteristics. Using an example, explain why each of the following characteristics of a loss exposure tends to make it possible to provide insurance.

   a.   Losses that involve pure risk

b. Losses that are accidental

c. Losses that are definite and measurable

d. Large number of similar exposure units

e. Losses that are not catastrophic

f. Loss exposures that are economically feasible to insure

3-2. Loss exposures must be definite and measurable to be insurable.

   a.   Give an example of an occurrence that could be insured.

   b.   Give an example of an occurrence that could *not* be insured.

3-3. Explain how an insurer can offer windstorm coverage and avoid the financial difficulty that a major windstorm can cause.

Application Question

3-4. Grocery Store is a chain of 100 large grocery stores. Annually, Grocery Store receives 500 complaints regarding dents that customers receive on their vehicles from grocery carts in the parking lot. The grocery carts are used carelessly by customers who allow them to roll into vehicles in the parking lot, causing scratches and dents. The average damage for each loss is $75. Do these losses exhibit the characteristics of an ideally insurable loss exposure?

Educational Objective 4
Describe the types of property and liability deductibles.

Key Words and Phrases

Deductible

Flat deductible

Disappearing deductible

Percentage deductible

Aggregate annual deductible

Per claim deductible

Per accident or per occurrence deductible

Waiting period

Review Questions

4-1. Explain how deductibles support the economical operation of insurance.

4-2. Briefly describe how these types of deductibles are applied in property insurance policies:

a. Flat, or straight, deductible

b. Disappearing, or franchise, deductible

c. Percentage deductible

d. Aggregate annual deductible

4-3. Briefly describe how these types of liability deductibles are applied in insurance policies:

a. Per claim deductible

b. Per accident/occurrence deductible

c. Waiting period deductible

Application Question

4-4. An earthquake causes a $3 million property loss to Office Building Company's
(OBC) building that was valued at $5 million before the loss. OBC's property
insurance policy has a $4.5 million coverage limit and contains a percentage
deductible (10 percent) that applies to the property's value at the time of the
loss. What is the dollar amount of OBC's deductible?

Educational Objective 5
Describe the purpose, operation, advantages, and disadvantages of large deductible plans.

Key Words and Phrases
Large deductible plan

Self-insurance

Residual market loading

Review Questions

5-1. Distinguish between a large deductible plan and a self-insured retention (SIR plan).

5-2. Describe two alternative means an insurer uses to recover the expenses it incurs to adjust losses under a large deductible plan.

5-3. Identify the advantages and disadvantages of large deductible plans.

Educational Objective 6
Explain why organizations need excess and/or umbrella liability insurance.

Key Word or Phrase

Underlying insurance

Review Questions

6-1. How do liability loss exposures differ from property loss exposures with regard to assessment of maximum possible loss?

6-2. Why is commercial liability insurance often arranged in "layers"?

6-3. How do aggregate limits of liability affect a commercial entity's need for liability insurance?

Educational Objective 7
Describe the basic differences between excess liability insurance and umbrella liability insurance.

Key Words and Phrases

Excess liability policy

Umbrella liability policy

Review Questions

7-1. Why are excess liability policies and umbrella liability policies used?

7-2. What is the basic difference between an excess liability policy and an umbrella liability policy?

7-3. List two reasons why, in actual practice, the distinction between excess and umbrella liability coverage is often unclear.

Educational Objective 8
Describe the different types of excess liability insurance and how each operates.

Key Words and Phrases
Self-contained excess liability policy

Aggregate, or stop loss, excess liability insurance policy

Review Questions

8-1.   Identify the three forms that an excess liability insurance policy may take.

8-2.   Under what circumstance will a following-form excess liability policy cover a claim in excess of the underlying limits?

8-3.   Explain why coverage gaps may occur between the excess and underlying layers when a self-contained excess liability policy is used.

8-4.   Identify a distinguishing feature of a true umbrella policy.

8-5. Contrast a specific excess liability policy with an aggregate excess liability policy.

Educational Objective 9
Explain how excess and umbrella liability insurance can be used in a layered liability insurance program, and describe the problems that may occur.

Key Words and Phrases

Working layers

Buffer layer

Review Questions

9-1. Explain the difference between working layers and buffer layers of insurance.

9-2. What are three problems that can occur when liability insurance is layered?

9-3. How do risk managers usually deal with the fact that there is no monetary limit on the amount a jury might award?

Educational Objective 10
Describe the options for structuring an international insurance program.

Key Words and Phrases

Admitted insurer

Nonadmitted insurer

Exporters package policy

Controlled master program

Economy of scale

Review Questions

10-1. Describe the advantages of purchasing admitted coverage locally.

10-2. Describe who the exporters package policy is intended for.

10-3. Describe who the admitted policies of a controlled master program cover.

10-4. Identify the primary advantage of a controlled master program.

Application Question

10-5. Joan is a risk management professional working for the parent company of a multinational corporation. She is trying to decide whether she should buy admitted or nonadmitted insurance to cover her employer's foreign subsidiary. Last year she purchased coverage from an admitted insurer. In that year, major claims went unpaid because of the insolvency of the insurer. The insurer also disputed the validity of the claims, saying Joan had misinterpreted the policy, which was written in the language of the country where the foreign subsidiary was domiciled. How will last year's lack of coverage likely influence Joan's decision to buy coverage from an admitted versus a nonadmitted insurer?

Answers to Assignment 3 Questions

NOTE: These answers are provided to give students a basic understanding of acceptable types of responses. They often are not the only valid answers and are not intended to provide an exhaustive response to the questions.

Educational Objective 1

1-1. Pooling reduces risk when the pooled losses are independent (or uncorrelated). Losses are independent if they are not subject to a common cause of loss.

1-2. Pooling does not change accident frequency or severity, but it does change the probability distribution of losses.

1-3. When losses are positively correlated, their distribution has a greater variability (higher standard deviation), and average losses are more difficult to predict.

1-4. Insurance and pooling differ in these ways: Insurance transfers risk from the insured to the insurer in exchange for premiums, and the insurer has additional financial resources from which it can fund losses.

1-5. In addition to risk transfer, insurers may offer risk control services (identifying loss exposures and recommending ways to control the associated risk) and claim and legal services (settling claims, administering claim payments, and preventing fraud; managing medical and disability claims; providing systems to report, track, and pay for claims; and providing legal expertise and a network of legal resources).

1-6. These answers address the Kendall Bus Company case:

a. A correlated loss exposure is one that would affect all of the buses simultaneously; for example, a design defect could require that all of Kendall's buses be repaired. An uncorrelated loss exposure would not affect all of the buses simultaneously; for example, a serious traffic accident would cause physical damage to a single bus.

b. Assuming both Kendall's and Green's buses included the same defective buses (a correlated loss), the risks would be unchanged. Regarding accident damage to one of Kendall's buses, pooling would not change the frequency or severity of serious accidents to which Kendall is exposed, but the overall cost of accidents would become more predictable, and Kendall's risk would be reduced.

c. A pool with fifteen other school bus companies would further reduce Kendall's risk involving uncorrelated loss exposures.

Educational Objective 2

2-1.   Insurance benefits individuals, organizations, and society in these ways:

- Indemnifies individuals and organizations for covered losses

- Enables individuals and organizations to manage cash flow uncertainty

- Enables individuals and organizations to meet legal requirements

- Promotes risk control

- Frees up insured's financial resources for other expenditures or investments

- Supports insured's credit

- Provides source of investment funds for insurers and insureds

- Helps reduce social burden

2-2.   Insurance helps an organization achieve risk financing goals in these ways:

- Indemnifies for covered losses—Insurance indemnifies the insured, subject to applicable deductibles and policy limits, for losses to covered loss exposures resulting from covered causes of loss.

- Manages cash flow uncertainty—Insurance helps reduce the financial effect on the insured's cash flow to any deductible payments and any loss amounts that exceed the policy limits.

- Meets legal requirements—Insurance is often used or required to satisfy statutory requirements and contractual requirements that arise from business relationships.

2-3.   These risk-sharing mechanisms promote risk control:

- Deductibles

- Premium credit incentives

- Contractual requirements

Educational Objective 3

3-1.   The type of insurance selected for discussion is auto liability coverage. The characteristics of auto liability that make it an ideally insurable loss exposure include the following:

   a.   It involves pure risk because there is no possibility of gain.

   b.   Losses are accidental; therefore, the insured generally has no incentive to cause an intentional auto liability loss to a third party.

   c.   Losses are definite and measurable, such as costs to repair or replace damage to a car and the cost of medical expenses.

   d.   Because most drivers need auto coverage, there are a large number of similar exposure units.

   e.   Losses are not catastrophic. Auto liability losses are independent—a liability loss suffered by one insured does not generally affect any other insureds.

    f. Losses are economically feasible to insure because an auto liability loss has a low probability of occurrence as well as the potential for high severity.

3-2. These answers address questions regarding the insurability of loss exposures.

    a. An example of an occurrence that could be insured would be the sudden bursting of a water pipe that causes water damage in the insured's bathroom.

    b. An example of an occurrence that could not be insured would be a slow leak in a bathroom pipe that causes decay and rotting of the insured's floor over several years.

3-3. An insurer can offer windstorm coverage and avoid the financial difficulty that a major windstorm can cause by diversifying the homes and businesses it insures so that it does not have a heavy concentration of insureds in any one geographical area.

3-4. To answer the question, you must compare Grocery Store's loss exposure to the characteristics of an ideally insurable loss exposure:

- Pure, not speculative risk: There is a possibility of a loss or no loss, but no possibility of gain.

- Similar exposure units: Yes, the loss exposures appear to be similar.

- Accidental: From Grocery Store's perspective, the losses are accidental in nature.

- Definite and measurable: Yes, the losses are definite in time and have measurable outcomes.

- Not catastrophic: The losses are not catastrophic in nature.

- Economically feasible to insure: The losses are relatively small and are highly probable. For this reason, this is probably not an ideally insurable loss exposure.

Educational Objective 4

4-1. Deductibles support the economical operation of insurance by allowing an insured organization to obtain the risk transfer it needs while retaining those losses it can safely absorb.

4-2. These answers describe how various deductibles are applied in property insurance policies:

    a. Flat, or straight, deductible—Stated in a dollar amount and usually applies per occurrence, regardless of the number of items of covered property that are damaged.

    b. Disappearing, or franchise, deductible—Decreases in amount as the amount of loss increases, and disappears entirely after a specified amount of loss is surpassed.

    c. Percentage deductible—Stated as a specified percentage of the loss, of the amount of insurance on the affected property, or of the value of the affected property.

    d. Aggregate annual deductible—Limits the total amount of losses retained during a year. After the aggregate annual deductible has been met, the insurer provides first-dollar coverage on all subsequent losses.

4-3. These answers describe how various liability deductibles are applied in insurance policies:

    a. Per claim deductible—applies to all damages sustained by any one person or organization as a result of one occurrence

b. Per accident/occurrence deductible—applies only once to the total of all claims paid arising out of one accident or occurrence

c. Waiting period deductible—payable after a specified time period

4-4. In the earthquake case involving OBC, OBC would retain $500,000 (10 percent of $5 million). This percentage deductible applies to the property's value at the time of the loss.

Educational Objective 5

5-1. Both large deductible and SIR plans require the insured organization to retain a relatively large amount of loss. A key difference is that, with a SIR, the insured organization is responsible for adjusting and paying its own losses up to the SIR amount.

5-2. Under a large deductible plan, the amount that the insurer incurs to adjust losses can be inside or outside the deductible. If they are inside, or included, the insurer adds them to the amount of the loss for the purpose of determining the total amount that is subject to the deductible. If they are outside, they are not added to the amount of the loss for the purpose of determining the amount subject to the deductible and are usually prorated between the insured and the insurer based on the size of the loss.

5-3. The advantages of large deductible plans are that they dramatically reduce the cost of risk compared with other insurance plans by avoiding a substantial amount of premium taxes, residual market loadings, and insurer overhead and profit charges. A large deductible plan also allows the insured organization to benefit from the cash flow on reserves for retained losses. The principal disadvantage of a large deductible plan is that losses may be higher than expected, lowering an organization's net income and cash flow.

Educational Objective 6

6-1. Estimating the maximum possible loss for a liability loss exposure is much harder than it is for a property loss exposure. Juries can award far larger judgments than anyone might have predicted.

6-2. To obtain the limits of liability insurance it deems desirable, a business might have to purchase several excess or umbrella liability policies.

6-3. Several claims in the policy period could exhaust the aggregate limits of a primary policy, in which case the insured would have no primary coverage for additional claims against that policy. The insured needs some way of covering this possibility.

Educational Objective 7

7-1. Excess liability policies and umbrella liability policies can be used to insure liability loss exposures that are too severe to be adequately covered under primary liability policies.

7-2. The coverage provided by an excess liability policy is no broader (and might be narrower) than that of the underlying insurance. An umbrella liability policy ordinarily provides broader coverage than the underlying and therefore could cover some claims not covered by the primary.

7-3. These are two reasons why the distinction between excess and umbrella liability coverage is often unclear:

- Courts and many in the insurance profession use the terms interchangeably.

- Many insurers providing excess and umbrella liability insurance do not use standardized policies.

Educational Objective 8

8-1. An excess liability insurance policy may take any of three basic forms:

- A following-form policy subject to the same provisions as the underlying policy

- A self-contained policy subject to its own provisions only

- A combination of these two types

8-2. A following-form excess liability policy will cover a claim in excess of the underlying limits only if the loss is covered by the underlying insurance.

8-3. Coverage gaps may occur between the excess and underlying layers when a self-contained excess liability policy is used because a self-contained excess liability policy does not depend on the provisions of the underlying policies for determining the scope of coverage (except when specifically written to cover exhausted underlying limits). A self-contained excess liability policy applies to a loss that exceeds the limits of the underlying policy only if the loss is also covered under the provisions of the self-contained excess liability policy.

8-4. One distinguishing feature of a true umbrella policy is a provision stating that the policy applies over a self-insured retention if the underlying policy does not cover a loss covered by the umbrella.

8-5. A specific excess liability policy requires the insured to retain a stipulated amount of loss from the first dollar for all losses resulting from a single occurrence. An aggregate excess liability policy requires the insured to retain a specified amount of loss from the first dollar during a specified period of time, usually one year.

Educational Objective 9

9-1. Primary and umbrella layers are generally referred to as the working layers, because they are the layers most often called on to pay claims. In some cases, an insured must purchase a buffer layer of excess insurance between the primary layer and the umbrella policy. This approach is used when the umbrella insurer will not provide coverage unless the insured has underlying coverage limits higher than those that the primary insurer is willing to provide.

9-2. These problems can occur when liability insurance is layered:

- Application of aggregate limits may vary in each layer.

- The excess policies may differ as to defense coverage.

- Excess layers over the first umbrella layer may purport to be following-form policies but in fact may contain restrictions not present in the umbrella layer.

9-3. Risk managers of large corporations commonly buy the highest limits they can obtain and hope that those limits will be adequate.

Educational Objective 10

10-1. These are the advantages of purchasing admitted coverage locally:

- The policy will be serviced locally, and local management is more likely accustomed to local practices.

- Premiums paid to admitted insurers are tax deductible as a business expense, while those paid to an insurer that is not admitted may not be tax deductible.

- Premiums and claims are paid in the local currency, which eliminates foreign exchange rate risks unless purchases must be on imported equipment or materials.

- Local agents and brokers may be able to understand local coverage nuances and provide better coverage advice.

- Complying with local laws and doing business locally helps integrate the company into the local economy and community.

10-2. The exporters package policy is intended for an insured without a permanent office or place of business in the foreign country where it operates.

10-3. The admitted policies of a controlled master program cover the foreign subsidiaries of a multinational business.

10-4. The primary advantage of a controlled master program is the prevention of gaps in coverage. What the local policy doesn't cover, the master policy may cover.

10-5. The two obstacles to coverage for last year's claims could be addressed by purchasing coverage through a nonadmitted insurer. The two advantages of nonadmitted insurance that are highly relevant to Joan's situation are:

- The financial strength of the insurer is more easily determined.

- The policy is written in the language of the country where the parent company is domiciled, making it easier to understand and administer.

These are disadvantages of nonadmitted insurance that Joan should also consider:

- Claim adjusting can be substantially more complicated without local coverage and local insurer representatives; this can be especially prominent with liability claims.

- Local management may not have confidence in the nonadmitted coverage provided by the parent company's insurer and may decide to buy its own coverage locally.

However, the disadvantages are likely to appear relatively minor to Joan when compared to not having any coverage for major claims last year.

Direct Your Learning

4

Self-Insurance Plans

After learning the content of this assignment, you should be able to:

1. Describe the purpose and operation of self-insurance plans.
2. Describe the two types of self-insurance plans.
3. Describe the administration of individual self-insurance plans.
4. Describe the advantages and disadvantages of self-insurance plans.
5. Given a case, justify a self-insurance plan that can meet an organization's risk financing needs.

Outline

▶ **Purpose and Operation of Self-Insurance Plans**
   A. Purpose of Self-Insurance Plans
   B. Operation of Self-Insurance Plans

▶ **Types of Self-Insurance Plans**
   A. Individual Self-Insurance Plans
   B. Group Self-Insurance Plans

▶ **Administration of Individual Self-Insurance Plans**
   A. Funding
   B. Record keeping
   C. Claim Settlement
   D. Loss Reserves
   E. Litigation Management
   F. Regulatory Filings
   G. Taxes, Assessments, and Fees
   H. Excess Liability Insurance

▶ **Advantages and Disadvantages of Self-Insurance Plans**
   A. Advantages of Self-Insurance Plans
   B. Disadvantages of Self-Insurance Plans

▶ **Selecting a Self-Insurance Plan**
   A. Case Facts
   B. Overview of Steps
   C. Step 1: Meeting the Requirements of a Self-Insurance Plan
   D. Step 2: Analyzing the Advantages and Disadvantages of a Self-Insured Plan
      1. Advantages
      2. Disadvantages

Use the SMART Online Practice Exams to test your understanding of the course material. You can review questions over a single assignment or multiple assignments, or you can take an exam over the entire course.

For each assignment, you should define or describe each of the Key Words and Phrases and answer each of the Review and Application Questions.

Educational Objective 1
Describe the purpose and operation of self-insurance plans.

Key Word or Phrase

Informal retention

Review Questions

1-1. Describe the purpose of a self-insurance plan.

1-2. Explain why high-severity losses are unsuitable for self-insurance.

1-3. Describe the organizations and types of losses for which self-insurance is most appropriate.

Educational Objective 2
Describe the two types of self-insurance plans.

Key Words and Phrases
Individual self-insurance plan

Group self-insurance plan

Review Questions

2-1. Identify the types of individual self-insurance plans that are generally subject to state regulatory control.

2-2. Distinguish between the loss exposures covered by individual self-insurance plans and those covered by group self-insurance plans.

2-3. Describe how a group self-insurance plan operates.

Educational Objective 3
Describe the administration of individual self-insurance plans.

Key Words and Phrases
Third-party administrator (TPA)

Incurred but not reported (IBNR) losses

Review Questions

3-1. List examples of activities that may be performed by a claim representative in the process of claim settlement for a self-insured organization.

3-2. Identify the conditions set forth in generally accepted accounting principles (GAAP) relating when a loss reserve must be established.

3-3. Identify the activities involved in litigation management.

3-4. Identify two approaches states use to assess self-insured organizations.

Application Question

3-5. Three Rivers Bicycle Manufacturing Company (TRB) self-insures its general liability loss exposure. Based on its extensive loss history, TRB's management directs the establishment of a $5 million expense on its income statement as well as a liability on its balance sheet. TRB's certified public accountant (CPA) objects. Explain the likely basis of the CPA's objection.

Educational Objective 4

Describe the advantages and disadvantages of self-insurance plans.

Review Questions

4-1. List the major advantages of self-insurance plans.

4-2. Explain how the use of a self-insurance plan encourages loss control.

4-3. Explain why an organization's long-run costs using self-insurance tend to be lower than the cost of transfer.

4-4. List the major disadvantages of self-insurance.

Application Question

4-5. National Home Builder (NHB) borrows millions of dollars annually from many financial institutions to finance its nationwide home-building operation. Identify one advantage and one disadvantage NHB should consider when evaluating self-insurance as a way to finance its loss exposures, and explain how each would apply specifically to NHB. (Answers may vary).

Educational Objective 5
Given a case, justify a self-insurance plan that can meet an organization's risk financing needs.

Application Question

5-1. ABC is a financially sound company that sells products around the country. It ships its products to customers using its own fleet of trucks. ABC management wants Sue, its risk management professional, to study whether the company should self-insure its fleet liability bodily injury claims, as it already self-insures its fleet liability property damage claims. Management thinks it is currently paying too much for this coverage and is convinced that this is because its insurer does not completely recognize ABC's superior loss control efforts. Bodily injury liability losses to third parties generally have low frequency and high severity. ABC's insurer charges an average of $2 million a year in premium to cover these losses. ABC's chief financial officer (CFO) assures Sue the company will set aside the amount it normally would pay its insurer in premium to pay for next year's losses and the cost to administer the self-insurance plan. Sue predicts the losses will be $1.5 million and that the cost to administer the plan will be $300,000 next year.

Use the case facts of ABC to answer the following questions.

a. Can ABC meet the requirements to implement a self-insurance pan? Explain your answer.

b.   What are the advantages to ABC of self-insuring its fleet liability claims for bodily injury? Explain your answer.

c.   What are the disadvantages to ABC of self-insuring its fleet liability claims for bodily injury? Explain your answer.

Answers to Assignment 4 Questions

NOTE: These answers are provided to give students a basic understanding of acceptable types of responses. They often are not the only valid answers and are not intended to provide an exhaustive response to the questions.

Educational Objective 1

1-1. The purpose of a self-insurance plan is to enable an organization to lower its long-term cost of risk by allowing it to pay for its own losses without incurring the transaction costs associated with insurance.

1-2. High-severity losses are unsuitable for self-insurance because they are typically low frequency and therefore relatively unpredictable, as well as too large to retain.

1-3. Self-insurance is most appropriate for organizations that are committed to risk control, able to tolerate risk retention, and willing to devote capital and resources to the program's financing and administration. Self-insurance is particularly suited for financing losses that can be budgeted and paid out over time, such as workers compensation, general liability, automobile liability, auto physical damage, professional liability, and flood and earthquake losses.

Educational Objective 2

2-1. Generally, only workers compensation, auto liability, and general liability self-insurance plans are subject to state regulatory control.

2-2. Individual self-insurance plans can be used with several types of loss exposures. Group self-insurance plans can be used only for workers compensation loss exposures and healthcare benefits.

2-3. A group self-insurance plan operates like an insurer in that it pools the loss exposures of its members. The plan's administrator issues member agreements, collects premiums, and manages claims. The administrator also purchases excess liability insurance (or excess of loss reinsurance) and makes required state regulatory filings.

Educational Objective 3

3-1. In the process of a claim settlement, a claim representative may investigate an accident scene, verify a claimant's statement of salary with the claimant's employer, and compare a claimant's statement of the circumstances surrounding an accident with the police report's description. When new information contradicts previously known information, a claim representative reexamines all of the information and investigates further to resolve the conflict or to determine which information is most credible. To determine the value of a loss, a claim representative usually consults numerous sources of information, such as valuation guides and records of prior claims with similar characteristics. To negotiate a claim settlement, the claim representative must have a thorough grasp of all the associated facts and communicate effectively.

3-2. GAAP requires the establishment of a loss reserve when (1) the loss occurred before the date of the financial statements and (2) the amount that will be paid on the loss can be reasonably estimated.

3-3. Litigation management involves these activities:

- Evaluating and selecting defense lawyers

- Supervising defense lawyers during litigation

- Keeping records of defense lawyer costs

- Auditing legal bills and evaluating alternative fee-billing strategies

3-4. States may assess taxes based on a percentage of losses or as a percentage of what the organization would have paid in premium.

3-5. The basis of the CPA's objection may be that, under GAAP, a self-insured organization cannot post loss reserves as a liability on its balance sheet and as an expense on its income statement if the losses have not occurred. If the organization were able to do this, it could later use those reserves and prematurely charge expenses to offset a year with higher-than-normal self-insured losses.

Educational Objective 4

4-1. The major advantages of self-insurance plans are these:

- Control over claims

- Loss control

- Long-term cost savings

- Cash flow benefits

4-2. Using a self-insurance plan encourages loss control because the organization directly pays the cost of its own losses and therefore has an incentive to prevent and reduce them and because, by doing so, it saves the associated loss payments and the expense of settling the claims.

4-3. An organization's long-run costs using self-insurance tend to be lower than the cost of transfer because the organization does not have to contribute to an insurer's overhead costs and profits, does not have to pay an insurer's risk charge, and is not subject to premium taxes and residual market loadings.

4-4. Major disadvantages of self-insurance include these:

- Uncertainty of retained loss outcomes

- Administrative requirements

- Deferral of tax deductions

- Contractual requirements

4-5. The fact that the cash flow generated by self-insurance results in retained losses that are paid over time is an advantage NHB should consider because of its extensive borrowing needs. NHB should consider the disadvantage of the administrative burden of self-insuring because the company operates in multiple states and must be aware of and comply with filing regulations in all states in which it operates.

Educational Objective 5

5-1. These answers address the ABC case:

a.   These are requirements of a self-insurance plan:

- Self-insuring a type of loss that is predictable

- Having sufficient financial resources and risk tolerance to retain potentially significant losses

- Having the organization willing to commit capital and resources to administer a self-insured plan

- Having the organization embrace loss control as part of its corporate culture

  Because fleet liability bodily injury claims to ABC generally have low frequency and high severity, Sue will have difficulty predicting future losses with high credibility, thereby increasing ABC's uncertainty and making these losses less suitable for retention. However, since ABC is financially sound, it may have sufficient financial resources and risk tolerance to retain potentially significant losses.

  In addition to guaranteeing the amount needed to pay expected losses, the CFO assured Sue that ABC will set aside $300,000 to administer the self-insurance plan. This action demonstrates that ABC is willing to commit capital and resources to administering such a plan.

  ABC management's belief that its insurer will never completely recognize ABC's superior loss control effort indicates that ABC believes in loss control. It is also evidence that loss control has become an essential part of ABC's corporate culture.

b.   These are the major advantages for ABC to use a self-insurance plan instead of insurance:

- Control over claims

- Loss control

- Long-term cost savings

- Cash flow benefits

  Control over claims allows ABC to set specific guidelines for adjusting losses. Claims can be minimized or eliminated through loss control. A self-insurance plan for ABC would allow the company to directly pay the costs of its own losses, creating a financial incentive for it to prevent or reduce them.

  Long-term costs of a self-insurance plan tend to be lower than the cost of risk transfer. The lower costs of the plan are a result of not having to contribute to an insurer's overhead costs and profits.

ABC's insurance premiums are due at the beginning of the covered time period. In comparison, its retained losses are not payable until they occur and are adjusted, which may result in payment many years after an insurance premium is due. Accordingly, under a self-insurance plan, ABC would retain use of the $2 million insurance premium until it is needed to pay losses and administrative costs as they are incurred throughout the coverage period. Liability claims can take years to be reported and years more to settle.

c. These are the major disadvantages for ABC to use a self-insurance plan instead of insurance:

- Uncertainty of retained loss outcomes

- Administrative requirements

- Deferral of tax deductions

- Contractual requirements

    Generally, one of the most important disadvantages of self-insuring is the uncertainty of retained losses. If ABC's retained losses are more frequent or severe than Sue initially expected, its earnings, net worth, and cash flow could be negatively affected.

    The administrative requirements of self-insurance are another disadvantage, particularly with liability claims. Reserving losses are more complex than with property claims because liability claims involve estimating the bodily injury and property damage losses of an adverse party. Further, reserving for a liability loss is often not a one-time event. For example, as new medical information comes in, the reserve for bodily injury liability must be reevaluated. There are likely regulatory filing requirements with government entities because these claims involve auto liability.

    Under a self-insurance plan, tax deductions are deferred; ABC would be allowed a tax deduction only as losses are paid out, rather than as they are incurred. In contrast, tax deduction for paying an insurance premium is allowed in the same year it is paid.

    Contractual requirements are likely not a major source of concern to ABC with its fleet liability bodily injury claims.

B

Assignment 5
Retrospective Rating Plans

Assignment 6
Reinsurance

Assignment 7
Captive Insurance

Assignment 8
Contractual Risk Transfer

Direct Your Learning ▶▶

Retrospective Rating Plans

Educational Objectives

After learning the content of this assignment, you should be able to:

1. Describe the purpose and operation of retrospective rating plans.

2. Given a case, calculate the premium for a retrospective rating plan.

3. Describe the following types of retrospective rating plans:
   - Incurred loss retrospective rating plan
   - Paid loss retrospective rating plan

4. Describe the administration of retrospective rating plans.

5. Describe the advantages and disadvantages of retrospective rating plans.

6. Given a case, justify a retrospective rating plan that can meet an organization's risk financing needs.

Outline

▶ **Purpose and Operation of Retrospective Rating Plans**

  A. Lines of Business and Characteristics of Losses

  B. Premium Determination

    1. Comparing Guaranteed-Cost and Retrospective Rating Insurance Plan Premiums

    2. Retrospective Rating Versus Experience Rating

    3. Maximum and Minimum Premiums

    4. Other Costs Incorporated Into the Premium

▶ **Calculating a Retrospective Rating Plan Premium**

  A. Retrospective Rating Premium Formula

    1. Standard Premium

    2. Basic Premium

    3. Converted Losses

    4. Excess Loss Premium

    5. Tax Multiplier

    6. Maximum and Minimum Premiums

    7. Premium Adjustments

  B. Retrospective Rating Plan Premium Calculation Case Study

    1. Case Facts

    2. Analysis

    3. Periodic Audits

▶ **Types of Retrospective Rating Plans**

  A. Incurred Loss Retrospective Rating Plan

  B. Paid Loss Retrospective Rating Plan

  C. Comparison of Paid Loss With Incurred Loss Retrospective Rating Plans

▶ **Administration of Retrospective Rating Plans**

  A. Collateral Requirements

  B. Financial Accounting Issues

  C. Tax Treatment

  D. Exit Strategy

▶ **Advantages and Disadvantages of Retrospective Rating Plans**

  A. Advantages of Retrospective Rating Plans

  B. Disadvantages of Retrospective Rating Plans

▶ **Selecting a Retrospective Rating Plan**

  A. Case Facts: Etchley Manufacturing

B. Steps in Evaluating Retrospective Rating Plans

  1. Determining Which Coverages to Include in the Retrospective Rating Plan

  2. Determining the Limit to Which the Retrospective Rating Plan Applies

  3. Determining the Loss Limitation

  4. Determining the Maximum and Minimum Premiums

  5. Evaluating the Maximum and Minimum Premium Choices

The SMART Online Practice Exams can be tailored to cover specific assignments, so you can focus your studies on topics you want to master.

For each assignment, you should define or describe each of the Key Words and Phrases and answer each of the Review and Application Questions.

Educational Objective 1
Describe the purpose and operation of retrospective rating plans.

Key Words and Phrases

Retrospective rating plan

Experience rating

Maximum premium

Minimum premium

Loss limit

Review Questions

1-1. Describe the lines of business that are typically covered under retrospective rating plans.

1-2. Contrast experience rating with retrospective rating.

1-3. Identify the costs that are incorporated into a retrospective rating plan premium.

Educational Objective 2
Given a case, calculate the premium for a retrospective rating plan.

Key Words and Phrases

Basic premium

Insurance charge

Converted losses

Loss conversion factor

▶▶

Excess loss premium

Tax multiplier

Review Questions

2-1. Explain what standard premium represents in the calculation of retrospective rating plan premium.

2-2. Describe the significance of a high loss conversion factor in relation to calculating a retrospective rating plan premium.

2-3. Describe the process of adjusting premium in a retrospective rating plan over time.

Application Question

2-4. Assume Northern Consolidated Technology (NCT) has these cost factors for its incurred loss retrospective rating plan:

Policy Limit—$1,000,000 per occurrence

Standard Premium—$500,000

Discount—$25,000

Basic Premium—20%

Loss Conversion Factor—1.10

Loss Limit—$500,000 per occurrence

Excess Loss Premium—5%

Tax Multiplier—1.04

Maximum Premium—150%

Minimum Premium—40%

a. Calculate NCT's basic premium.

b. Calculate NCT's excess loss premium.

c. Calculate NCT's maximum and minimum premiums.

Educational Objective 3

Describe the following types of retrospective rating plans:

- **Incurred loss retrospective rating plan**
- **Paid loss retrospective rating plan**

Key Words and Phrases

Incurred loss retrospective rating plan

Paid loss retrospective rating plan

Review Questions

3-1. Distinguish between an incurred loss retrospective rating plan and a paid loss retrospective rating plan.

3-2. Describe the advantage to an insured organization of using a paid loss retrospective rating plan rather than an incurred loss retrospective rating plan.

3-3. Explain why an organization might favor an incurred loss retrospective rating plan over a paid loss retrospective rating plan, despite the advantage discussed in the preceding question.

Application Question

3-4. East Side Manufacturing Company has a workers compensation insurance policy under a retrospective rating plan from Bellingham Insurance. The policy period began on February 1. On June 27, an accident at the plant seriously injures seven of East Side's employees. Bellingham investigates the accident, but because of the case's complexity, several years pass before it is settled. Following settlement, Bellingham assesses a fee against East Side. Explain why this happens, and identify the type of retrospective rating plan East Side has.

Educational Objective 4
Describe the administration of retrospective rating plans.

Review Questions

4-1. Identify the administrative duties performed by the following entities under a retrospective rating plan:

a. The insurer

b. The insured

4-2. Explain why many insurers using a paid loss retrospective rating plan require the insured organization to provide collateral.

4-3. Identify the financial accounting issues an insured organization considers when using a retrospective rating plan.

Application Question

4-4. At the end of its policy year, an organization with a paid loss retrospective rating plan has $75,000 in paid losses and $450,000 in incurred losses. Based on its incurred losses, its retrospective rating premium is $550,000. For financial accounting purposes, identify the expense figure the organization should use on its income statement at the end of the policy period.

Educational Objective 5
Describe the advantages and disadvantages of retrospective rating plans.

Review Questions

5-1. Identify two advantages of a retrospective rating plan over a guaranteed-cost insurance plan.

5-2. Identify three possible disadvantages of a retrospective rating plan compared with a guaranteed-cost plan.

5-3. Identify a potential objection to the insurer's premium adjustment process under retrospective rating plans.

Application Question

5-4. Metal Etching Company's (MEC) risk management professional believes that MEC's future workers compensation losses will be minimal because the company's new manufacturing process uses microbes to engrave metal instead of acid. Consequently, the risk management professional has proposed that MEC purchase a retrospective rating plan with low minimum premiums, high maximum premiums, and no loss limitation. Describe the worst-case scenario under the proposed retrospective rating plan.

Educational Objective 6

Given a case, justify a retrospective rating plan that can meet an organization's risk financing needs.

Application Question

6-1. Green Mountain Demolition, Inc. (GMD), specializes in demolishing multiple-story buildings with explosives and removing the resulting debris from building sites. GMD's workforce fluctuates between thirty-five and sixty employees because of the seasonal nature of the work. The business also owns fifteen dump trucks and six automobiles. Because of the hazards involved, GMD has significant loss exposures for both workers compensation and general liability.

GMD's current insurance coverage includes a retrospective rating plan for its workers compensation coverage and guaranteed-cost coverages for its other exposures, including its liability exposure. In the past three years, five lawsuits have been filed against GMD because of damage to buildings near demolition sites caused by the shock of explosions. The company's management has researched and adopted corrective measures that they believe will minimize such damage in the future; however, the company's liability coverage premiums have increased significantly because of the lawsuits. GMD's risk manager is looking for ways to reduce insurance expenses and is considering expanding its workers compensation retrospective rating plan to cover additional exposures.

a. GMD's risk manager is considering adding GMD's building and personal property loss exposures; auto collision damage, medical payments, and liability exposures; and general liability exposures to the retrospective rating plans. Identify which exposures are mostly likely to be included under a retrospective rating plan, and explain your answer.

b. Explain why GMD's risk manager might consider applying a loss limit to the retrospective rating plan.

c. GMD's insurer has suggested minimum and maximum premiums for the retrospective rating plan. The risk manager is willing to accept a high minimum premium to reduce insurance costs, but he wants to present a case for a lower maximum premium. Identify a factor on which the risk manager may base his case for a lower maximum premium.

Answers to Assignment 5 Questions

NOTE: These answers are provided to give students a basic understanding of acceptable types of responses. They often are not the only valid answers and are not intended to provide an exhaustive response to the questions.

Educational Objective 1

1-1. Organizations commonly use retrospective rating plans for losses arising from their liability loss exposures that are covered by workers compensation, auto liability, and general liability insurance policies. Organizations can also use retrospective rating plans for auto physical damage, crime, and glass loss exposures.

1-2. Experience rating adjusts the premium for the current policy period to recognize the loss experience of the insured organization during past policy periods. In contrast, retrospective rating plans adjust the premium for the current policy period to recognize the insured's loss experience during the current policy period. The insured organization's past loss experience is not completely ignored in the retrospective rating plan because past loss experience is reflected in the standard premium. However, past lost experience is less important relative to current losses.

1-3. Other than retained losses, costs incorporated into a retrospective rating plan premium include insurer overhead and profits, residual market loadings, premium taxes, and a risk transfer premium.

Educational Objective 2

2-1. Standard premium, the amount an insured organization pays for insurance coverage under a guaranteed-cost insurance plan, reflects a combination of industry-wide loss experience for a class of organizations (exposure rating) and the insured's actual loss experience (experience rating).

2-2. A high loss conversion factor implies that there is a high cost for the insurer to provide claims services for which the cost is not allocated to individual claims. Consequently, a retrospective rating plan with a high loss conversion factor is more expensive for the insured organization than one with a lower loss conversion factor.

2-3. The initial standard premium for a retrospective rating plan is based on estimated exposures. Sometime after the end of the policy period, the insurer adjusts the standard premium based on actual exposures for the policy period. At about the same time (after the end of the policy period), the insurer applies the retrospective rating premium formula to the adjusted standard premium, considering the insured organization's incurred losses (paid and reserved losses) for the policy period. The result is an adjusted retrospective rating plan premium that also accounts for what the insured organization has already paid in premium.

In subsequent periods, usually annually, further adjustments are made to the retrospective rating plan premium by applying the retrospective rating premium formula to subsequent evaluations of incurred losses that occurred during the policy period. If the evaluation of incurred losses for the policy period shows an increase in cumulative incurred losses from one adjustment to the next, an additional premium is due. If the evaluation shows that cumulative incurred losses for the policy period have decreased, premium is returned to the insured organization. This series of premium adjustments continues until all retained losses are paid or until the insurer and the insured organization agree that no further retrospective rating premium adjustments are required.

2-4. The following answers provide calculations for NCT's retrospective rating plan:

    a. NCT's basic premium: Standard premium × Basic premium percentage

        $500,000 × 20% = $100,000

    b. NCT's excess loss premium: Standard premium × Excess loss premium factor percentage × Loss conversion factor

        $500,000 × 5% × 1.10 = $27,500

    c. NCT's maximum premium: Standard premium × Maximum premium percentage

        $500,000 × 150% = $750,000

        NCT's minimum premium: Standard premium × Minimum premium percentage

        $500,000 × 40% = $200,000

Educational Objective 3

3-1. With an incurred loss retrospective rating plan, an insured organization pays a deposit premium during the policy period. After the end of the policy period, the insurer adjusts the premium based on the insured organization's actual incurred losses. With a paid loss retrospective rating plan, the insured organization pays a deposit premium at the beginning of the policy period and reimburses the insurer for its losses as the insurer pays for them.

3-2. Under a paid loss retrospective rating plan, the insured organization benefits from the cash flow available on the funds it retains rather than paying them to the insurer. Relative to an incurred loss retrospective rating plan, the insurer generally requires a smaller deposit premium, thereby further enhancing the insured organization's cash flow.

3-3. Under a paid loss retrospective rating plan, an insurer usually adds an amount to the basic premium to compensate itself for not having use of the cash flow on the loss reserves. Therefore, the insured should not automatically choose a paid loss plan over an incurred loss plan, because the decision depends on the relationship between the amount that the insurer adds to the basic premium and the value of the cash flow benefit to the insured.

3-4. In the East Side Manufacturing Company case, the fee represents the premium assessed from Bellingham for payment of losses resulting from the accident. East Side has a paid loss plan, under which it pays a deposit premium at the beginning of the policy period and reimburses Bellingham for its losses as the insurer pays for them, subject to minimum and maximum premiums.

Educational Objective 4

4-1. These answers identify the entities' duties under a retrospective rating plan:

    a. The insurer is responsible for many of the tasks of administering retrospective rating plans, such as adjusting losses, making necessary filings with state regulatory authorities, and paying applicable premium taxes and residual market loadings.

b.   The insured organization's responsibility is limited to making premium payments and arranging for any required security (collateral), such as letters of credit, to guarantee future loss payments.

4-2.   Many insurers using a paid loss retrospective rating plan require the insured organization to provide collateral to guarantee that future premium adjustments will be paid.

4-3.   An insured organization considers these financial accounting issues when using a retrospective rating plan:

- Future premium payments should be posted as a liability on the insured's balance sheet and charged as an expense on its income statement.

- Any additional premium for incurred but not reported retained losses should be posted as a liability on the insured's balance sheet and as an expense on its income statement.

4-4.   For financial accounting purposes, the organization should use $550,000 for its expense figure on its income statement at the end of the policy period.

Educational Objective 5

5-1.   Two advantages of a retrospective rating plan over a guaranteed-cost insurance plan are that its long-run cost tends to be lower than the cost of transfer and that it encourages risk control because of the direct link between losses and premium.

5-2.   Possible disadvantages of a retrospective rating plan compared with a guaranteed-cost plan are these:

- If not properly designed, a retrospective rating plan can make financial planning difficult for the insured organization.

- If the insurer sets unrealistically high reserves for the retained portion of losses, the insured organization would pay a premium based on inflated loss reserve figures, resulting in a loss of cash flow.

- The losses ultimately retained by the insured organization are initially paid to the insurer as a premium. Because of this, the losses must be increased so that the insurer can pay premium taxes and residual market loadings.

5-3.   A potential objection to the insurer's premium adjustment process under retrospective rating plans is that an insurer may not diligently adjust losses when it knows the insured organization is retaining them, resulting in loss payments that are higher than necessary.

5-4.   MEC's risk management professional may be wrong about MEC's future losses. In a worst-case scenario, MEC could incur losses equal to or greater than those incurred in the past. For example, the company has workers compensation exposures other than those related to the engraving process and may have unforeseen exposures related to the new process. With no loss limitation and a high maximum premium, MEC's retrospective rating premium could be substantially larger than expected.

Educational Objective 6

6-1. The following answers are based on the Green Mountain Demolition case.

a. Retrospective rating plans are usually used with workers compensation but may combine loss exposures for auto liability and general liability. Coverages for other exposures are uncommon. Therefore, GMD could most likely add its auto liability and general liability exposures to a retrospective rating plan but not its building and personal property, auto collision damage, or auto medical payments exposures.

b. GMD's risk manager might consider applying a loss limit to the retrospective rating plan because doing so would reduce the retrospective plan premium.

c. GMD's risk manager might base his case for a lower maximum premium on the fact that the company has adopted corrective measures that should eliminate or minimize lawsuits for damage to neighboring buildings from the shock of demolition explosions; therefore, the company's expected losses could be significantly lower than in past years. (Research data to support the premise would strengthen his position.)

Direct Your Learning

6

Reinsurance

After learning the content of this assignment, you should be able to:

1. Describe reinsurance and its principal functions.

2. Describe the three sources of reinsurance.

3. Describe treaty reinsurance and facultative reinsurance.

4. Describe the types of pro rata reinsurance and excess of loss reinsurance and their uses.

5. Explain the reinsurance concerns of risk management professionals.

Outline

▶ **Reinsurance and Its Functions**

  A. Basic Terms and Concepts

  B. Reinsurance Functions

    1. Increase Large-Line Capacity

    2. Provide Catastrophe Protection

    3. Stabilize Loss Experience

    4. Provide Surplus Relief

    5. Facilitate Withdrawal From a Market Segment

    6. Provide Underwriting Guidance

▶ **Reinsurance Sources**

  A. Professional Reinsurers

  B. Reinsurance Departments of Primary Insurers

  C. Reinsurance Pools, Syndicates, and Associations

  D. Reinsurance Professional and Trade Associations

    1. Intermediaries and Reinsurance Underwriters Association (IRU)

    2. Brokers & Reinsurance Markets Association (BRMA)

    3. Reinsurance Association of America (RAA)

▶ **Reinsurance Transactions**

  A. Treaty Reinsurance

  B. Facultative Reinsurance

▶ **Types of Reinsurance**

  A. Pro Rata Reinsurance

    1. Quota Share Reinsurance

    2. Surplus Share Reinsurance

  B. Excess of Loss Reinsurance

    1. Per Risk Excess of Loss

    2. Catastrophe Excess of Loss

    3. Per Policy Excess of Loss

    4. Per Occurrence Excess of Loss

    5. Aggregate Excess of Loss

▶ **Reinsurance Concerns of Risk Management Professionals**

  A. Portfolio Reinsurance Arrangements

  B. Cut-Through Endorsements

  C. Reinsurance Through a Subsidiary

  D. Reinsuring a Pool

  E. Cooperation Between Insurers and Reinsurers to Provide Capacity

s.m.a.r.t. tips

When you take the randomized full practice exams in the SMART Online Practice Exams product, you are seeing the same kinds of questions you will see when you take the actual exam.

For each assignment, you should define or describe each of the Key Words and Phrases and answer each of the Review and Application Questions.

Educational Objective 1
Describe reinsurance and its principal functions.

Key Words and Phrases

Reinsurance

Primary insurer

Reinsurer

Reinsurance agreement

Insurance risk

Retention

Reinsurance premium

Ceding commission

Retrocession

Retrocedent

Retrocessionaire

Large-line capacity

Line

Surplus relief

Policyholders' surplus

Portfolio reinsurance

Novation

Review Questions

1-1. Briefly define reinsurance.

1-2. Describe the purpose of a retrocession.

1-3. Describe some of the practical business goals that reinsurance can help an insurer achieve.

1-4. List the six principal functions that reinsurance performs for primary insurers.

1-5. Describe how increasing its large-line capacity allows an insurer to grow.

1-6.   Name the three ways in which a primary insurer can use reinsurance to stabilize its loss experience.

1-7.   Explain how a primary insurer may completely eliminate the liabilities it has assumed under the policies it has issued.

Educational Objective 2
Describe the three sources of reinsurance.

Key Words and Phrases

Professional reinsurer

Direct writing reinsurer

Reinsurance intermediary

Reinsurance pools, syndicates, and associations

Reinsurance pool

Syndicate

Association

Review Questions

2-1. Identify the three sources from which reinsurance may be purchased.

2-2. Describe the role of a reinsurance intermediary.

2-3. Name the factors a primary insurer should evaluate when considering a reinsurer.

2-4. Describe the function of reinsurance pools, syndicates, and associations.

2-5. List three of the most widely known reinsurance professional and trade associations.

Educational Objective 3
Describe treaty reinsurance and facultative reinsurance.

Key Words and Phrases

Treaty reinsurance

Facultative reinsurance

Adverse selection

Facultative certificate of reinsurance

Review Questions

3-1. Contrast treaty reinsurance and facultative reinsurance.

3-2. Explain why primary insurers usually make treaty reinsurance agreements so their underwriters do not have to exercise discretion in using reinsurance.

3-3. Identify the four functions of facultative reinsurance.

Educational Objective 4
Describe the types of pro rata reinsurance and excess of loss reinsurance and their uses.

Key Words and Phrases

Pro rata reinsurance

Loss adjustment expense (LAE)

Flat commission

Profit-sharing commission

Sliding scale commission

Quota share reinsurance

Loss ratio

Catastrophe excess of loss reinsurance

Variable quota share treaty

Surplus share reinsurance

Bordereau

Line guide

Excess of loss reinsurance (nonproportional reinsurance)

Attachment point

Subject premium

Working cover

Per risk excess of loss reinsurance

Loss occurrence clause

Per policy excess of loss reinsurance

Per occurrence excess of loss reinsurance

Clash cover

Extracontractual damages

Excess of policy limits loss

Aggregate excess of loss reinsurance

Review Questions

4-1. Identify the two basic types of reinsurance transactions.

4-2. Identify the two principal approaches that reinsurers use to allocate losses.

4-3. Describe the distinguishing characteristic of quota share reinsurance.

4-4. Explain how the amount of insurance, the premium, and losses are allocated under a pro rata reinsurance agreement.

4-5. Describe the distinguishing characteristic of surplus share reinsurance.

4-6. Describe the circumstance in which a reinsurer will respond to a loss under an excess of loss reinsurance agreement.

4-7. Describe the two most common approaches to handling loss adjustment expenses under an excess of loss reinsurance agreement.

4-8. Describe the application of per risk excess of loss reinsurance.

4-9. Describe how a loss occurrence clause functions within a catastrophe excess of loss reinsurance agreement.

4-10. Describe the purpose of catastrophe excess of loss reinsurance.

4-11. Explain how per policy excess of loss reinsurance functions.

4-12. Explain how per occurrence excess of loss reinsurance functions.

4-13. Describe the types of liability insurance for which clash cover is useful.

4-14. Describe the type of losses that aggregate excess of loss reinsurance covers.

Educational Objective 5
Explain the reinsurance concerns of risk management professionals.

Key Word or Phrase

Cut-through endorsement

Review Questions

5-1. Identify situations in which a risk management professional would deal directly with a reinsurer.

5-2. Explain why a risk management professional whose insurance plan has been reinsured through a portfolio reinsurance arrangement should be aware of details of the transaction.

5-3. Identify the factors a risk management professional should consider when reinsuring risk through a pool.

Answers to Assignment 6 Questions

NOTE: These answers are provided to give students a basic understanding of acceptable types of responses. They often are not the only valid answers and are not intended to provide an exhaustive response to the questions.

Educational Objective 1

1-1. Reinsurance is the transfer from one insurer to another of some or all of the financial consequences of certain loss exposures covered by the primary insurer's policies.

1-2. Under a retrocession, one reinsurer, the retrocedent, transfers all or part of the reinsurance risk that it has assumed or will assume to another reinsurer, the retrocessionaire.

1-3. Reinsurance helps an insurer achieve several practical business goals, such as insuring large exposures, protecting policyholders' surplus from adverse loss experience, and financing the insurer's growth.

1-4. Although several of its uses overlap, reinsurance is a valuable tool that can perform six principal functions for primary insurers:

   • Increase large-line capacity

   • Provide catastrophe protection

   • Stabilize loss experience

   • Provide surplus relief

   • Facilitate withdrawal from a market segment

   • Provide underwriting guidance

1-5. Increasing large-line capacity allows a primary insurer to assume more significant risks than its financial condition and regulations would otherwise permit.

1-6. A primary insurer can stabilize loss experience by obtaining reinsurance to accomplish any, or all, of these purposes:

   • Limit its liability for a single loss exposure

   • Limit its liability for several loss exposures affected by a common event

   • Limit its liability for loss exposures that aggregate claims over time

1-7. A primary insurer can completely eliminate the liabilities it has assumed under the insurance policies it has issued through a novation. A novation is not considered portfolio reinsurance because the substitute insurer assumes the direct obligations to insureds covered by the underlying insurance.

Educational Objective 2

2-1. Reinsurance can be purchased from three sources:

- Professional reinsurers

- Reinsurance departments of primary insurers

- Reinsurance pools, syndicates, and associations

2-2. Reinsurance intermediaries generally represent a primary insurer and work with that insurer to develop a reinsurance program that is then placed with a reinsurer or reinsurers.

2-3. The primary insurer should evaluate the reinsurer's claim-paying ability, reputation, and management competence before entering into the reinsurance agreement.

2-4. Reinsurance pools, syndicates, and associations provide member companies the opportunity to participate in a line of insurance with a limited amount of capital—and a proportionate share of the administrative costs—without having to employ the specialists needed for such a venture.

2-5. Three of the most widely known reinsurance professional and trade associations are these:

- Intermediaries and Reinsurance Underwriters Association (IRU)

- Brokers & Reinsurance Markets Association (BRMA)

- Reinsurance Association of America (RAA)

Educational Objective 3

3-1. In treaty reinsurance, the reinsurer agrees in advance to reinsure all the loss exposures that fall within the treaty. Although some treaties allow the reinsurer limited discretion in reinsuring individual loss exposures, most treaties require that all loss exposures within the treaty's terms must be reinsured.

In facultative reinsurance, the primary insurer negotiates a separate reinsurance agreement for each loss exposure that it wants to reinsure. The primary insurer is not obligated to purchase reinsurance, and the reinsurer is not obligated to reinsure loss exposures submitted to it.

3-2. Primary insurers usually make treaty reinsurance agreements so their underwriters do not have to exercise discretion in using reinsurance. If treaty reinsurance agreements permitted primary insurers to choose which loss exposures they ceded to the reinsurer, the reinsurer would be exposed to adverse selection.

3-3. Facultative reinsurance serves these four functions:

- Facultative reinsurance can provide large line capacity for loss exposures that exceed the limits of treaty reinsurance agreements.

- Facultative reinsurance can reduce the primary insurer's exposure in a given geographic area.

- Facultative reinsurance can insure a loss exposure with atypical hazard characteristics and thereby maintain the favorable loss experience of the primary insurer's treaty reinsurance and any associated profit-sharing arrangements.

- Facultative reinsurance can insure particular classes of loss exposures that are excluded under treaty reinsurance.

Educational Objective 4

4-1. The two basic types of reinsurance transactions are treaty reinsurance and facultative reinsurance.

4-2. The principal approaches that reinsurers use to allocate losses are broadly defined as pro rata reinsurance and excess of loss reinsurance.

4-3. The distinguishing characteristic of quota share reinsurance is that the primary insurer and the reinsurer use a fixed percentage in sharing the amounts of insurance, policy premiums, and losses (including loss adjustment expenses).

4-4. Under a pro rata reinsurance agreement, the amount of insurance, the premium, and the losses (including loss adjustment expenses) are divided between the primary insurer and the reinsurer in the same proportions as the risk.

4-5. The distinguishing characteristic of surplus share reinsurance is that when an underlying policy's total amount of insurance exceeds a stipulated dollar amount, or line, the reinsurer assumes the surplus share of the amount of insurance (the difference between the primary insurer's line and the total amount of insurance).

4-6. In an excess of loss reinsurance agreement, also called "non-proportional reinsurance," the reinsurer responds to a loss only when the loss exceeds the primary insurer's retention, often referred to as the attachment point.

4-7. These are the two most common approaches to handling loss adjustment expenses:

- Prorate the loss adjustment expenses between the primary insurer and the reinsurer based on the same percentage share that each is responsible for the loss

- Add the loss adjustment expenses to the amount of the loss when applying the attachment point of the excess of loss reinsurance agreement

4-8. Per risk excess of loss reinsurance applies separately to *each loss* occurring to *each risk*, with the primary insurer usually determining what constitutes one risk (loss exposure).

4-9. A loss occurrence clause specifies a time period, in hours, during which the primary insurer's losses from the same catastrophic occurrence can be aggregated and applied to the attachment point and reinsurance limits of the catastrophe excess of loss reinsurance agreement. Such clauses usually specify a time period of 72 consecutive hours (3 days) for hurricane losses and 168 consecutive hours (7 days) for earthquake losses.

4-10. Catastrophe excess of loss reinsurance protects the primary insurer from an accumulation of retained losses that arise from a single catastrophic event.

4-11. Per policy excess of loss reinsurance is used primarily with liability insurance. It applies the attachment point and the reinsurance limit separately to each insurance policy issued by the primary insurer, regardless of the number of losses occurring under each policy.

4-12. Per occurrence excess of loss reinsurance applies the attachment point and the reinsurance limit to the total losses arising from a single event affecting one or more of the primary insurer's policies.

4-13. Clash cover may be useful for types of liability insurance in which loss adjustment expenses are likely to be very high and the underlying per occurrence reinsurance limits include these expenses rather than prorate them.

4-14. Aggregate excess of loss reinsurance can be used for property or liability insurance and covers aggregated losses that exceed the attachment point and occur over a stated period, usually one year.

Educational Objective 5

5-1. These are situations in which a risk management professional would deal directly with a reinsurer:

- A reinsurer takes the place of an insurer as a result of a portfolio reinsurance arrangement.

- A reinsurer takes the place of an insurer through a cut-through endorsement added to an insurance policy.

- An organization establishes a subsidiary that insures or reinsurers the organization's loss exposures.

- An organization purchases reinsurance for a pool of which it is a member.

- A reinsurer or several reinsurers team up with an insurer or several insurers to provide coverage.

5-2. A risk management professional whose insurance plan has been reinsured through a portfolio reinsurance arrangement should learn the details of the transaction in order to ascertain that coverage is maintained and that the reinsurer is at least as financially sound as the retiring insurer.

5-3. Factors a risk management professional should consider when reinsuring risk through a pool are the financial strength, integrity, and operating efficiency of the pool's reinsurer, which all affect the pool's reliability and the solidarity and effectiveness of the organization's risk financing program.

Direct Your Learning

Captive Insurance

Educational Objectives

After learning the content of this assignment, you should be able to:

1. Describe the purpose and characteristics of captive insurance plans.

2. Describe the types of captive insurance plans available.

3. Describe the advantages and disadvantages of using a captive insurance plan.

4. Describe the following considerations for forming and operating a captive insurance plan:

   - Conducting a feasibility study

   - Operating as a reinsurer or a direct writing captive insurer

   - Selecting lines of business

   - Setting premium arrangement

   - Determining captive domicile

Outline

▶ **Purpose and Characteristics of Captive Insurance Plans**

  A. Retaining and Transferring Losses

  B. Combining a Captive Insurance Plan With Transfer and Hybrid Risk Financing Plans

▶ **Types of Captive Insurance Plans**

  A. Single-Parent (or Pure) Captive

  B. Group Captive

  C. Risk Retention Group

  D. Agency Captive

  E. Rent-a-Captive

  F. Protected Cell Company

▶ **Advantages and Disadvantages of Using a Captive Insurance Plan**

  A. Advantages of a Captive Insurance Plan

    1. Reducing the Cost of Risk

    2. Benefiting From Cash Flow

    3. Obtaining Insurance Not Otherwise Available

    4. Having Direct Access to Reinsurers

    5. Negotiating With Insurers

    6. Centralizing Loss Retention

    7. Obtaining Potential Cash Flow Advantages on Income Taxes

    8. Controlling Losses

    9. Obtaining Rate Equity

  B. Disadvantages of a Captive Insurance Plan

    1. Capital and Start-Up Costs

    2. Sensitivity to Losses

    3. Pressure From Parent Company Management

    4. Premium Taxes and Residual Market Loadings

▶ **Formation and Operation of Captive Insurance Plans**

  A. Conducting a Feasibility Study

  B. Operating as a Reinsurer or a Direct Writing Captive Insurer

  C. Selecting Lines of Business

  D. Setting Premium Arrangement

  E. Determining Captive Domicile

Narrow the focus of what you need to learn. Remember, the Educational Objectives are the foundation of the course, and the exam is based on these Educational Objectives.

For each assignment, you should define or describe each of the Key Words and Phrases and answer each of the Review and Application Questions.

Educational Objective 1
Describe the purpose and characteristics of captive insurance plans.

Key Word or Phrase

Captive insurer, or captive

Review Questions

1-1. Describe how aggregate excess of loss reinsurance relates to captive insurance plans.

1-2. Describe how a captive insurance plan works with a hybrid or transfer plan.

1-3. Explain why a captive insurance plan is often a hybrid risk financing plan.

Application Question

1-4. Fairfield, Inc., has a captive insurance plan with a $2 million per occurrence layer of loss. The captive insurer purchases excess of loss reinsurance of $1 million excess of $300,000 per occurrence. Fairfield purchases excess insurance on a guaranteed-cost basis with a limit of $30 million per occurrence.

    a.   Determine the total limit of insurance available to Fairfield per occurrence.

    b.   Identify the amounts per occurrence retained by both Fairfield and its captive and the amount that would be transferred to reinsurers through the captive.

Educational Objective 2
Describe the types of captive insurance plans available.

Key Words and Phrases

Single-parent captive (pure captive)

Group captive

Association captive

Risk retention group

Agency captive

Rent-a-captive

Protected cell company (PCC)

Review Questions

2-1. Explain why a single parent captive is a hybrid refinancing plan.

2-2. Describe a major benefit of a risk retention group.

2-3. Describe a major benefit of a rent-a-captive.

Educational Objective 3
Describe the advantages and disadvantages of using a captive insurance plan.

Key Words and Phrases

Risk shifting

Risk distribution

Review Questions

3-1. Describe how a captive insurance plan can help an organization reduce its cost of risk.

3-2. Describe how having direct access to reinsurers can benefit a captive insurer.

3-3. Explain why retention of losses is a disadvantage for a captive insurer.

Application Question

3-4. An architectural firm is considering joining an association captive. However, its senior partners are reluctant to sever a long-standing relationship with the firm's insurance agent, whom they believe has negotiated to the best of his abilities to obtain an acceptable rate from the firm's professional liability insurer. The partners decide to retain a quota share percentage of its liability insurance and to insure the rest through the commercial insurer. They believe this approach will give them two advantages when dealing with the commercial insurer. Describe those advantages.

Educational Objective 4

Describe the following considerations for forming and operating a captive insurance plan:

- **Conducting a feasibility study**
- **Operating as a reinsurer or a direct writing captive insurer**
- **Selecting lines of business**
- **Setting premium arrangement**
- **Determining captive domicile**

Key Words and Phrases

Fronting company

Direct writing captive insurer

Review Questions

4-1. Describe the focus and prelude for a feasibility study of a captive insurance plan.

4-2. Describe the major elements of a feasibility study of a captive insurance plan.

4-3. Describe an advantage to an organization of having its captive operate as a reinsurer and as a direct writing captive insurer.

4-4. Describe the lines of business typically covered by captive insurance plans.

4-5. Compare guaranteed-cost and retrospectively rated premium arrangements between the parent and captive insurer for captive insurance plans.

4-6. List five of the factors an organization should consider when evaluating a domicile for a captive insurer.

Application Question

4-7. An organization enters into a captive insurance arrangement with a fronting company for an incurred loss retrospective rating plan with a loss limit of $500,000 per occurrence for its workers compensation loss exposures. The captive insurer then purchases excess of loss reinsurance of $1,000,000 for any loss in excess of $1,000,000 per occurrence. What is the captive insurer's net loss exposure per occurrence (aside from minimum and maximum premium considerations)?

Answers to Assignment 7 Questions

NOTE: These answers are provided to give students a basic understanding of acceptable types of responses. They often are not the only valid answers and are not intended to provide an exhaustive response to the questions.

Educational Objective 1

1-1. Aggregate excess of loss reinsurance is usually difficult to obtain, even in a soft market, so most captive insurers do not purchase it. If the captive insurer can purchase aggregate excess of loss reinsurance, then its annual retained losses are capped at an annual maximum amount, similar in concept to a maximum premium under a retrospective rating plan.

1-2. When combined with a hybrid or transfer plan, a captive insurance plan generally is used for the first layer of losses, if a relatively high loss frequency and low-to-medium loss severity exist, and a transfer or hybrid plan covers the higher-severity losses.

1-3. A captive insurance plan is often a hybrid risk financing plan because its characteristics normally involve both retention and transfer. The severity of the losses covered by a captive insurer, because losses are partially retained, is typically low to moderate. Because a captive insurer acts as any other insurer does, the losses are funded.

1-4. These answers relate to Fairfield, Inc., and its captive insurer:

  a. The total limit of insurance available to Fairfield per occurrence is $32 million.

  b. Fairfield retains the first $300,000 per occurrence because its captive insurer retains $300,000 per occurrence, net of reinsurance. It also retains $700,000 excess of $1,300,000, for a total retention of $1,000,000.

Educational Objective 2

2-1. A single-parent captive is a hybrid refinancing plan because, from its parent's point of view, it usually combines elements of retention and transfer. Because a single-parent captive covers its parent's losses and is part of the same economic family as its parent, losses retained by the captive are, in effect, retained by its parent. For the same reasons, losses transferred by the captive insurer (for example, through reinsurance or some other means) are, in effect, transferred by its parent. Some single-parent captive insurers that do not purchase reinsurance retain all of their losses and therefore should not be considered a hybrid plan.

2-2. A major benefit of a risk retention group is that it needs to be licensed in only one state to provide liability coverage to group members anywhere in the United States. The U.S. Liability Risk Retention Act of 1986 supersedes state law that requires an insurer to be licensed in every state in which it sells insurance, thereby saving the risk retention group the expense of complying with regulations in each of the fifty states.

2-3. A major benefit of a rent-a-captive is that the renting organization receives credit for underwriting profits and investment income. Consequently, the organization benefits from using a captive insurer but is not required to invest its own capital. Each insured keeps its own premium and loss account, so no risk shifting or distribution occurs among the members of a rent-a-captive.

Educational Objective 3

3-1.   A captive insurance plan can help an organization reduce its cost of risk over the long run when compared with guaranteed-cost insurance because it involves retention; saves the acquisition costs of obtaining insurance; reduces underwriting expenses; saves the cost of the commercial insurer's overhead and profit; and allows for investment income from premium, loss reserve, and collateral investment dollars.

3-2.   A captive insurer provides the insured organization with direct access to the international market of reinsurers, which can be more flexible than insurers in terms of underwriting and rating. A captive insurer that uses reinsurance can capture any ceding commission on the reinsurance that would otherwise be paid to a commercial insurer. In addition, by removing the primary commercial insurer, the insured organization saves substantial markup costs.

3-3.   Retention of losses can be a disadvantage for a captive insurer, because if the losses retained are higher than forecasted and exceed allocated funds, the financial solvency of the captive could be threatened. Financial insolvency would then prevent payment of the parent company's losses.

3-4.   In relation to dealing with its commercial insurer, the firm gains two advantages by having a captive:

- Increased negotiating power—Because of limited competition in the market, the insurer may normally charge a high rate for professional liability insurance; however, if the firm has the option of increasing the share of liability coverage it places in its captive, it can try to negotiate a lower rate. The insurer, in turn, may agree to charge a lower premium to retain the firm's business.

- Rate equity—The firm's predicted losses based on historical data may indicate that it is paying higher-than-warranted premiums to the commercial insurer because of the poor loss histories of other firms with which it is pooled. In contrast, the captive has the rating flexibility to charge premiums that may more accurately reflect the firm's predicted losses. The commercial insurer may be less inclined to assess the firm a higher rate to compensate for other insureds' losses if it knows the firm can obtain a more equitable rate from the captive.

Educational Objective 4

4-1.   An effective feasibility study should focus on an organization's goals for the captive insurance plan. This allows the organization to optimize the plan's design. As a prelude to conducting the study, an organization's management should carefully consider the decision to enter a captive insurance plan: doing so involves a multiyear commitment of substantial administrative and capital resources that could be invested at potentially higher rates of return elsewhere.

4-2.   A feasibility study of a captive insurance plan should analyze the parent company's risk financing structure, including the type of insurance coverages used, the amounts of coverage purchased, retention levels, premiums paid, supporting collateral, and the type of rating plans applied. The study should then assess the exposure basis of the parent company, including sales, payroll, and property values. It must also assess losses and should create projected *pro forma* financial statements for the proposed captive.

4-3. By having its captive reinsure a fronting company, the insured can use a captive insurer and comply with licensing requirements. In addition, a captive insurer that reinsures a fronting company usually satisfies other parties—such as mortgagees, loss payees, and business partners—that require the insured organization to purchase insurance from an established insurer with an acceptable rating from one of the major rating agencies. By operating as a direct writing captive insurer, a captive can save an organization the fees charged by the fronting company, which can range from 5 percent to 30 percent of premium.

4-4. Captive insurance plans are commonly used to cover lines of business that offer substantial cash flow. A captive insurance plan allows the insured to benefit from the cash flow available on losses that are paid out over time because the captive earns investment income on premium funds that have not yet been paid out for claims, including loss reserves and unearned premiums. Lines of business that offer the greatest cash flow benefit are long-tail lines such as workers compensation, general liability, and automobile liability. Captives may also be used to cover certain types of property losses as well as losses that fall under specialized types of business, such as products and environmental liability.

4-5. Under a guaranteed-cost arrangement, the insured organization pays a fixed premium rate, transferring the entire loss exposure to its captive. If the premium arrangement is on a retrospectively rated basis, the premium rate adjusts based on a portion of the insured's covered losses during the policy period.

4-6. When evaluating a domicile for a captive insurer, the organization should consider these factors:

- Minimum premium requirements
- Minimum capitalization
- Solvency requirements
- Incorporation and registration expenses
- Local taxes
- Types of insurance that can be written
- General regulatory environment
- Investment restrictions
- Ease and reliability of communications and travel to and from the domicile
- Political stability
- Support infrastructure in terms of captive managers, claim administrators, bankers, accountants, lawyers, actuaries, and other services

4-7. The captive insurer's net loss exposure per occurrence is $1,000,000 if the loss does not exceed $2,000,000. The captive insurer purchased $1,000,000 of excess of loss reinsurance for any loss in excess of $1,000,000. Therefore, the reinsurer will pay any loss between $1,000,000 and $2,000,000. The captive insurer has exposure for the amount of any loss that exceeds $2,000,000, in addition to the net exposure of $1,000,000.

Direct Your Learning

8

Contractual Risk Transfer

Educational Objectives

After learning the content of this assignment, you should be able to:

1. Describe the types of contractual risk transfer for hazard risk.

2. Describe contractual risk transfer by type of transaction.

3. Explain how contractual risk transfer for hazard risk can alter common-law liabilities.

4. Describe the types of statutory limitations on hold-harmless agreements.

5. Explain how to manage contractual risk transfer for hazard risk.

Outline

▶ **Types of Contractual Risk Transfer**

  A. Types of Contractual Risk Transfer

  B. Noninsurance Risk Control Transfer

    1. Incorporation

    2. Leasing

    3. Contracting for Services

    4. Suretyship and Guaranty Agreements

    5. Waiver

    6. Limitation of Liability

    7. Disclaimer of Warranties

  C. Noninsurance Risk Financing Transfer

    1. Hold-Harmless Agreement

    2. Transfer of Risk to the Transferee's Insurer

▶ **Contractual Risk Transfer by Type of Transaction**

  A. Construction Contracts

  B. Service and Maintenance Contracts

  C. Purchase Order Contracts

  D. Lease of Premises Contracts

  E. Equipment Lease Contracts

  F. Bailment Contracts

  G. Sale and Supply Contracts

▶ **Contractual Risk Transfer of Common-Law Liabilities**

  A. Limited Form

  B. Intermediate Form

  C. Broad Form

▶ **Statutory Limitations on Hold-Harmless Agreements**

  A. All-Inclusive Statutes

  B. Statutes Prohibiting Particular Wording

  C. Statutes Placing Requirements on Agreements

▶ **Managing Contractual Risk Transfer**

  A. Legal and Practical Considerations

    1. Legal Enforceability

    2. Parties' Ability to Manage Risk

    3. Nature and Extent of Risk Transferred

  B. Strategic and Administrative Considerations

    1. Transfer Strategy

    2. General Administrative Controls

    3. Record Keeping

    4. Specific Control Measures

Studying before sleeping helps you retain material better than studying before undertaking other tasks.

For each assignment, you should define or describe each of the Key Words and Phrases and answer each of the Review and Application Questions.

Educational Objective 1
Describe the types of contractual risk transfer for hazard risk.

Key Words and Phrases

Noninsurance risk control transfer

Noninsurance risk financing transfer

Segregation

Leasehold

Sale-and-lease-back (sale-and-lease-back arrangement)

Surety

Obligee

Principal

Guarantor

Exoneration

Subrogation

Indemnity

Waiver

Exculpatory clause (exculpatory agreement)

Waiver of subrogation

Indemnitor

Indemnitee

Additional insured endorsement

Named insured endorsement

Review Questions

1-1. Describe the two categories of contractual risk transfer.

1-2. Describe how segregation works to insulate a corporation from potential losses.

1-3. Describe how each of these types of transactions transfers risk exposures:

a. Leasing

b. Suretyship agreements

    c.   Waivers

    d.   Disclaimers of warranties

1-4. Describe how each of these types of transactions transfers risk financing:

    a.   Hold-harmless agreement

    b.   Insurance agreements

Application Question

1-5. Sports Gear, Inc., manufactures sporting and exercise equipment. The equipment is assembled in health clubs and sports facilities by distributors. Sports Gear's risk management professional is looking for ways to reduce its products liability loss resulting from injuries caused by the machines. Recommend a contractual risk transfer option the risk management professional might consider.

Educational Objective 2
Describe contractual risk transfer by type of transaction.

Key Words and Phrases

Bailment

Mutual benefit bailment

Gratuitous bailment

Free on board (F.O.B.) point of origin

Free on board destination (FOB destination)

Cost, insurance, freight (CIF)

Installment or conditional sales contract

Fungible goods

Review Questions

2-1. Explain why a risk management professional should be aware of transfers of risk control or risk financing in an organization's contractual agreements.

2-2. Identify the types of contracts that may contain noninsurance transfers of risk control or risk financing.

2-3. Give examples of ways a bailee and a bailor may contractually alter their level of liability under a mutual benefit bailment.

2-4. Describe how the following contracts transfer risk between the buyers and sellers of goods:

    a.   Consignment

    b.   Conditional sales contract

Application Question

2-5. A manufacturer in Chicago shipped goods to a customer in Atlanta by truck. Three blocks from the customer's Atlanta location, the truck slid on ice and overturned, damaging the goods. Identify which party bears the loss under each of the following shipment terms.

    a.   F.O.B. Chicago

    b.   F.O.B. Atlanta

c. C.I.F.

Educational Objective 3
Explain how contractual risk transfer for hazard risk can alter common-law liabilities.

Key Word or Phrase

Vicarious liability

Review Questions

3-1. Describe the risks transferred under a limited form of hold-harmless agreement.

3-2. Describe the risks transferred under an intermediate form of hold-harmless agreement.

3-3. Describe the risks transferred under the broad form of hold-harmless agreement.

Educational Objective 4
Describe the types of statutory limitations on hold-harmless agreements.

Review Questions

4-1. Describe the effect of all-inclusive statutes that apply to hold-harmless agreements.

4-2. Describe the effect of statutes that prohibit particular wording of hold-harmless agreements.

4-3. Describe the effect of statutes that place requirements on hold-harmless agreements.

Educational Objective 5
Explain how to manage contractual risk transfer for hazard risk.

Review Questions

5-1. Describe briefly these three legal and practical considerations of contractual risk transfer:

   a.   Legal enforceability

   b.   Parties' ability to manage risk

   c.   Nature and extent of risk transferred

5-2. Contrast the defensive and offensive approaches to contractual risk transfer.

5-3. Describe the specific control measures that should be used when transferred loss exposures are to be covered by insurance.

Application Question

5-4. Northern Consolidated manufactures machines used by factories to assemble other machines. Northern ships the machine parts to independent distributors, who assemble the machines in customers' factories. Because of the expertise and liability exposures involved in assembling the machines, Northern is facing a shortage of distributors. Fairfield Machine Services has developed the expertise, and contract negotiations are proceeding for Fairfield to become a distributor.

Fairfield has proposed a clause in the contract under which Northern would assume all liability for losses resulting from defects in the machines. Northern's risk management professional has recommended against Northern's agreeing to this transfer. Explain why.

Answers to Assignment 8 Questions

NOTE: These answers are provided to give students a basic understanding of acceptable types of responses. They often are not the only valid answers and are not intended to provide an exhaustive response to the questions.

Educational Objective 1

1-1.   Contractual risk transfers fall into two categories:

- Noninsurance risk control transfer—When an organization contractually transfers risk control responsibilities to a party that is not an insurer, it essentially shifts the loss exposures associated with that risk to the transferee.

- Noninsurance risk financing transfer—When an organization contractually transfers the financial burden of losses, the underlying loss exposures are not transferred between the parties.

1-2.   A corporation's management can insulate the organization from potential losses by designating a separate corporation to conduct each of the organization's major activities. This practice is known as segregation. With segregation, the "divisions" between an organization's exposure units constitute the legal boundaries of separate corporations, thereby limiting loss potentials that arise from business risks, property losses, liability losses, and net income losses.

1-3.   These answers address how these transactions transfer risk exposures:

a.   An organization that leases property rather than owning it practices risk control by allowing the property owner to retain the risks related to property ownership.

b.   A surety's contractual guarantee is to perform or hire someone to perform in the principal's place when the principal's failure or inability to perform becomes clear and the obligee demands performance from the surety. A surety agreement protects the obligee by providing a second source of performance.

c.   An individual or organization can relinquish its right to sue in contract or tort using a waiver. By allowing an organization to rid itself of the applicable liability loss exposures, waivers can function as effective risk control mechanisms.

d.   A disclaimer in a sales contract may deny any express warranties made in conjunction with the property's sale. In addition, it may deny implied warranties, such as the implied warranty for a particular purpose—that the seller is aware of the particular purpose for which the buyer will use the property and that the property is suitable for that purpose—and the implied warranty of merchantability—that the property is suitable for the purpose for which most buyers use it.

1-4.   These answers address how the described transactions transfer risk financing:

a.   Under a hold-harmless agreement, one party agrees to assume the liability of a second party. The assuming party, or indemnitor, assumes liability for the legal claims that may be brought against the other party, the indemnitee, because of the activities the contract covers.

b. Insurance agreements can be modified to allow the transferee's insurer to treat a specified third party as an insured. This can be accomplished through two kinds of endorsements—additional insured and named insured—which obligate the transferee's insurer to pay (or pay on behalf of) the third party after it has suffered a loss.

1-5. Sports Gear's risk management professional might suggest inclusion in distributors' contracts of a hold-harmless clause under which the distributors agree to assume liability for injuries resulting from assembly of the equipment. Sports Gear may have sufficient bargaining power to require the distributors to assume the risk.

Educational Objective 2

2-1. A risk management professional should be aware of contractual transfers of risk control or risk financing contained in an organization's contractual agreements because they could contain conflicts that could render the transfers meaningless.

2-2. The following types of contracts may contain noninsurance risk transfers:

- Construction contracts

- Service and maintenance contracts

- Purchase order contracts

- Lease of premises contracts

- Equipment lease contracts

- Bailment contracts

- Sale and supply contracts

2-3. A bailee may seek to limit liability through posted notices or contract provisions stating it is not responsible for damage to a bailor's goods. A bailee may also attempt to limit liability to a specified amount per item or only to the value of the property. A bailor may seek to increase the bailee's liability by holding the bailee responsible for specified acts of God.

2-4. These answers relate to the transfer of risk between buyers and sellers of goods under specific types of contracts:

a. Consignment—Title to the property is placed with the manufacturer or processor until the distributor sells the goods to the retailer or ultimate consumer. The distributor is never exposed to loss from their damage or destruction.

b. Conditional sales contract—The seller usually retains title. Exposure to loss because of property damage can be transferred immediately to the buyer by the sales contract.

2-5. These parties bear the loss under the shipment terms:

a. F.O.B. Chicago—The manufacturer in Chicago is absolved of responsibility for the property once it has reached Atlanta; therefore, the customer bears the loss.

b. F.O.B. Atlanta—The manufacturer bears the loss because the shipment is still en route to its destination.

c.   C.I.F.—The customer in Atlanta acquired ownership of the goods as soon as they were loaded on the truck; however, as part of the C.I.F. agreement, the manufacturer would have purchased sufficient insurance to cover the loss.

Educational Objective 3

3-1.   Under the limited form of hold-harmless agreement, one party (the transferor) transfers its responsibility for the fault of the other party (the transferee) to that party.

3-2.   The intermediate form of hold-harmless agreement transfers the sole fault of the transferee as well as joint fault of the transferor and transferee.

3-3.   The broad form of hold-harmless agreement attempts to place all financial consequences of potential losses on the transferee—including losses resulting from the sole fault of the transferor.

Educational Objective 4

4-1.   An all-inclusive statute entirely prohibits transfer of risk, or virtually all hold-harmless agreements.

4-2.   Statutes that prohibit particular wording of hold-harmless agreements may prohibit a narrowly defined class of agreement—for example, those that transfer responsibility for losses resulting exclusively from a transferor's negligence—or they may address transfers of risk in specific types of contracts, such as building contracts or specifications for bids.

4-3.   Some states specify that if a particular type of contract does include a hold-harmless agreement, it must comply with certain requirements. For example, several states require hold-harmless agreements in construction and design contracts to include a monetary limit on the extent of the indemnification that bears a reasonable commercial relationship to the contract.

Educational Objective 5

5-1.   The following answers describe the legal and practical considerations of contractual risk transfer.

a.   A contract is not enforceable if it is unconscionable or in violation of public policy or statutes. Attempts by the contracting parties to rid themselves of the same or related loss exposures or financial consequences could make it difficult to enforce the contract. Contracts in which risks have been transferred and retransferred can make it almost impossible for a court to determine who has agreed to accept what risk and may be unenforceable as a result.

b.   The parties' ability to manage risk is a consideration of contractual risk transfer, particularly the transferee's ability to pay major losses when they occur. Generally, transferees must receive enough benefits from their contracts to cover the obligations assumed under them. Moreover, transfers could make it impractical to handle a loss exposure in a more efficient way or could even preclude such a possibility. For example, the transferee may be unable not only to pay for large losses but also to effectively reduce losses.

c.   The greatest efficiency is typically achieved when the responsibility for risk financing and the authority for risk control rest with the same party. Because dividing lines between responsibilities are not always clear, the underlying contract, in the interests of economy and ease of enforcement, should be specifically and carefully worded.

5-2.   A defensive approach to contractual risk transfer requires an organization to avoid inadvertently becoming a transferee. An offensive approach entails taking advantage of other organizations by wielding economic power to impose transfers.

5-3.   For loss exposures to be covered by insurance, the risk management professional must be as certain as possible that coverage is available either under the organization's current coverages or for purchase. The risk management professional must also examine the other contracting party's insurance protection, if any. Whether the exposure is covered under an existing policy or additional coverage will be purchased, the risk management professional should provide a clear description of the coverage that applies, including the insurer's legal defense obligations.

5-4.   The risk management professional would likely be concerned about the nature and extent of risk transferred. Under the proposed transfer agreement, Northern would assume liability arising out of Fairfield's assembly of the machines, even though that assembly is fully outside Northern's control and fully under Fairfield's control. The risk management professional may be particularly concerned about the possibility of negligence in the assembly of the machines. By transferring responsibility for the quality of the assembly work, Fairfield would have little incentive to control losses; Northern, although contractually responsible for such losses, would have no authority to control them.

Assignment 9
Transferring Financial Risk

Assignment 10
Transferring Hazard Risk to the Capital Markets

Assignment 11
Allocating Costs of Managing Hazard Risk

Direct Your Learning

Transferring Financial Risk

Educational Objectives

After learning the content of this assignment, you should be able to:

1. Describe the various types of financial risk.

2. Explain how an organization can use derivatives such as forwards, futures, options, and swaps to transfer financial risk.

3. Explain how an organization can use securitization to transfer financial risk.

4. Given information on an organization's financial risk, recommend ways to transfer the risk.

Outline

▶ **Types of Financial Risk**

    A. Market Risk

        1. Interest Rate Risk

        2. Exchange Rate Risk

        3. Liquidity Risk

    B. Credit Risk

    C. Price Risk

▶ **Derivatives**

    A. Forward Contracts

    B. Options

    C. Swaps

▶ **Securitization**

    A. Securitization

        1. Special Purpose Vehicle (SPV)

        2. Income-Producing Assets

        3. Securitization Model

        4. Regulatory Requirements

▶ **Transferring Financial Risk**

    A. Case Facts

    B. Overview of Steps

    C. Financial Risk in Raising Cash Through Debt

    D. Financial Risk in Raising Cash by Selling Accounts Receivable

    E. Financial Risk in Fluctuating Price of Special Fabric

Plan to register with The Institutes well in advance of your exam. For complete information regarding exam dates and fees, please visit our web page, www.TheInstitutes.org/forms, where you can access and print exam registration information.

For each assignment, you should define or describe each of the Key Words and Phrases and answer each of the Review and Application Questions.

Educational Objective 1
Describe the various types of financial risk.

Key Words and Phrases

Market risk

Interest rate risk

Exchange rate risk

Liquidity risk

Credit risk

Price risk

Review Questions

1-1. Describe a financial instrument.

1-2. Explain what uncertainty causes liquidity risk.

1-3. Describe output price risk.

Application Question

1-4. Sam is a plumber who fixed the water heater at Pete's house. Pete did not pay Sam at the time he did the repair work but promised he would within a couple of weeks. A month has passed, and Sam has become concerned he will not be paid. What risk is being described in this case?

Educational Objective 2
Explain how an organization can use derivatives such as forwards, futures, options, and swaps to transfer financial risk.

Key Words and Phrases

Forward contract

Call option

Put option

Review Questions

2-1. Describe several benefits of a forward contract that is exchange-traded.

2-2. Explain the difference between a call option and a put option.

2-3. Explain how counterparties to a swap usually structure the amount paid up front.

Application Question

2-4. Sam owns a lumber yard that sells lumber to home builders. He bought a put option that allows him to sell a large portion of his inventory at a strike price in six months. The following questions pertain to Sam's lumber.

a. If in six months the current market price of Sam's lumber is higher than the strike price of his put option, what will happen to the value of the option, and what will Sam likely do?

b. If in six months the current market price of Sam's lumber is lower than the strike price of Sam's put option, what will happen to the value of the option, and what will Sam likely do?

Educational Objective 3
Explain how an organization can use securitization to transfer financial risk.

Review Questions

3-1. Explain why special purpose vehicles (SPV) were established.

3-2. Describe a major benefit of involving an SPV in a securitization transaction.

3-3. Explain why regulators, auditors, and potential investors scrutinize the use of SPVs.

Application Question

3-4. Bejax sells industrial equipment in several foreign countries. Some customers in those countries are late in paying their bill from Bejax. Management of Bejax would like to convert its accounts receivable to cash so it can expand into new markets. Is securitization an option for Bejax? Explain your answer.

Educational Objective 4
Given information on an organization's financial risk, recommend ways to transfer the risk.

Key Words and Phrases

Option contract

Strike price

Application Question

4-1. Freckles Paint Store (FPS) must raise cash quickly to meet current financial obligations. Its management wants to raise cash using two methods. The first is to take out a loan, which it expects to pay off early, as it is able to obtain long-term financing at a reasonable interest rate. The second method of raising cash involves converting past sales into cash. Past sales have resulted in a large accounts receivable account, which contains the amounts due from customers that have not yet paid for the paint they bought. Several investors have expressed an interest in paying cash for FPS's accounts receivable; however, because of FPS's weak financial condition, no intermediary is willing to act as a special purpose vehicle (SPV) for the investors. The following questions relate to the FPS case:

a. Explain how being able to obtain long-term financing affects FPS's interest rate risk.

b. Explain how FPS's inability to find an SPV to help it convert its accounts receivable to cash assets will affect its credit risk.

Answers to Assignment 9 Questions

NOTE: These answers are provided to give students a basic understanding of acceptable types of responses. They often are not the only valid answers and are not intended to provide an exhaustive response to the questions.

Educational Objective 1

1-1.   A financial instrument is a check, a bond, a share of stock, or another document with monetary value. A financial instrument could also be a binding agreement between parties for payment of money.

1-2.   Liquidity risk involves the uncertainty over an organization having enough cash or other assets that can be converted to cash and maintain value should there be an immediate demand for cash.

1-3.   Output price risk is the uncertainty of what price the organization can charge for its product.

1-4.   Credit risk is being described. Also referred to as counterparty risk, it occurs due to the uncertainty about a party (Pete) who is obligated to pay money per a binding agreement. The uncertainty concerns whether Pete will actually pay all of the money he owes and pay it on time. Pete is obligated to pay as a customer who bought Sam's services on credit. If every customer paid the amount owed on time, there would be no credit risk. However, if Pete defaults on the credit agreement, the income from the sale of Sam's services is at risk.

Educational Objective 2

2-1.   A forward contract that is exchange-traded, or a futures contract, has the benefits of being standardized, openly available, and transferable.

2-2.   A call option is an option that gives the holder the right to buy an asset. A put option is an option that gives the holder the right to sell an asset.

2-3.   Swaps are frequently structured so that no money is paid up front between counterparties for the contract. Instead, cash flows are exchanged back and forth between the organizations throughout the term of the swap.

2-4.   These answers relate to the Sam's lumber yard case:

   a.   An option is an agreement that gives its holder the right, but not the obligation, to buy or sell an asset at a specific price over a period of time. In the case presented, Sam has the option to sell his lumber at a strike price over six months. Because the strike price is lower than the current market price, the value of the option is negligible, and Sam will likely not sell his lumber at the strike price. He can earn higher sales revenue by selling at the current market price.

   b.   Because in the scenario presented the strike price is higher than the current market price, Sam will likely sell his lumber at the strike price. He can earn higher sales revenue by doing this, as the value of the option is the difference between the strike price and the current market price.

Educational Objective 3

3-1. SPVs were established for the purpose of purchasing income-producing assets from an organization, holding title to them, and then using those assets to collateralize securities that will be sold to investors.

3-2. A major benefit of involving an SPV in a securitization transaction is that investors can decide whether to invest in the securities based solely on the risk presented by the income-producing assets held as collateral by the SPV.

3-3. Regulators, auditors, and potential investors scrutinize the use of SPVs because they have been used to manipulate organizations' income statements and balance sheets.

3-4. Yes, securitization is potentially an option. Bejax can use securitization to exchange income-producing assets for cash provided by the purchaser of the security, assuming that a market exists for the asset. This exchange allows Bejax to convert the asset to cash on its balance sheet. The special purpose vehicle (SPV) securitizes the accounts receivable by using them as collateral for securities it sells to investors. The SPV then uses the interest and principal repayments on the accounts receivable to fund the interest and principal repayments to the security investors. The securities carry the risks of the accounts receivable held by the SPV. These risks include the possibility of default by Bejax customers.

Educational Objective 4

4-1. These answers relate to the Freckles Paint Store (FPS) case:

a. If FPS had only been able to obtain short-term financing at a reasonable interest rate, it would have been concerned that when the time came to refinance the debt, the interest rate could rise, creating an expense that FPS could not afford. Because, in fact, FPS does not have to refinance the loan when it expires, this exposure to interest rate risk is lowered.

b. A major benefit of involving an SPV in a securitization transaction is that investors can decide whether to invest in the securities based solely on risk presented by the income-producing assets, or accounts receivable, held as collateral by the SPV. If FPS directly securitized its income-producing assets without using an SPV as an intermediary, investors would need to consider not only the risks presented by the income-producing assets, but also the overall credit risk of FPS. Analyzing overall credit risk is complex because FPS may hold many different types of assets and incur many different types of liabilities. Even expert investors have difficulty accurately analyzing such credit risk. An SPV reduces this associated credit risk; conversely, not having an SPV increases this associated credit risk.

Direct Your Learning

Transferring Hazard Risk to the Capital Markets

Educational Objectives

After learning the content of this assignment, you should be able to:

1. Describe the types of capital market products used for risk financing.

2. Explain how insurance-linked securities operate in terms of the following:
   - The use of catastrophe bonds
   - The benefits to investors
   - The advantages and disadvantages

3. Explain how insurance derivatives operate, including:
   - The use of swaps
   - The use of insurance options
   - The advantages and disadvantages of insurance derivatives

4. Explain how these contingent capital arrangements operate:
   - The use of a standby credit facility
   - The use of a contingent surplus note arrangement
   - The use of a catastrophe equity put arrangement
   - The advantages and disadvantages of contingent capital arrangements

5. Analyze the concerns of organizations that use insurance-linked securities and insurance derivatives to transfer risk and the investors supplying capital.

6. Describe the regulatory and accounting issues involved with insurance-linked securities and insurance derivatives.

Outline

▶ **Capital Market Risk Financing Products**

  A. Types of Capital Market Products

    1. Insurance-Linked Securities

    2. Insurance Derivatives

    3. Contingent Capital Arrangements

  B. Value of Capital Market Products

▶ **Insurance-Linked Securities**

  A. Operation of Insurance Securitizations

  B. Use of Catastrophe Bonds

  C. Benefits to Investors

  D. Advantages of Insurance Securitizations

    1. Create Additional Risk Transfer Capacity

    2. Lower Credit Risk

  E. Disadvantages of Insurance Securitizations

    1. Exposure to the Volatility of the Market's Demand

    2. Opportunity Cost of Collateralized Assets

    3. Transaction Costs

    4. Basis Risk

▶ **Insurance Derivatives**

  A. Use of Swaps

  B. Use of Insurance Options

  C. Advantages of Insurance Derivatives

  D. Disadvantages of Insurance Derivatives

▶ **Contingent Capital Arrangements**

  A. Standby Credit Facility

  B. Contingent Surplus Note

  C. Catastrophe Equity Put Option

    1. Advantages of Contingent Capital Arrangements

    2. Disadvantages of Contingent Capital Arrangements

▶ **Concerns of Users and Suppliers of Capital for Transferring Hazard Risk**

  A. Organizations Transferring Risk

    1. Securities and Options

    2. Structured Options and Insurance

    3. Standardized, Exchange-Traded Options

    4. Financial Security and No Basis Risk

  B. Investors Supplying Capital

▶ **Capital Market Regulatory and Accounting Issues**

Set aside a specific, realistic amount of time to study every day.

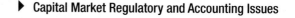

For each assignment, you should define or describe each of the Key Words and Phrases and answer each of the Review and Application Questions.

Educational Objective 1
Describe the types of capital market products used for risk financing.

Key Words and Phrases

Catastrophe

Capital market

Contingent capital arrangement

Securitization

Special purpose vehicle (SPV)

Derivative

Review Questions

1-1.   The most common insurance-linked security is a catastrophe bond. Describe how catastrophe bonds provide funds to offset losses.

1-2.   Explain how an insurance derivative can provide risk financing.

1-3.   Describe the features of a contingent capital arrangement and why it is different than risk transfer.

Educational Objective 2

Explain how insurance-linked securities operate in terms of the following:

- **The use of catastrophe bonds**
- **The benefits to investors**
- **The advantages and disadvantages**

Key Word or Phrase

Insurance-linked security

Review Questions

2-1. Explain how insurance securitization differs from most other types of securitization.

2-2. Explain the operation of catastrophe bonds.

2-3. Explain why some risk management professionals believe that the financial security provided by a typical insurance securitization is greater than that provided by a traditional insurance or reinsurance transaction.

Application Question

2-4. Valerie works as an investment broker for Arkwright Insurance Company. Arkwright is examining its options for securing losses above $10 million, as well as above $25 million, for the next three years. Arkwright's management is considering a two-tiered program based on a reinsurance contract to secure its losses of $10 million to below $25 million and then to purchase an insurance-linked security (ILS) for its losses that exceed $25 million. Considering that the underwriting cycle is entering the early phase of a soft cycle (with low competition and insurance rate declines) and stock prices are increasing rapidly, why might Valerie advise Arkwright against purchasing an ILS as part of its program?

Educational Objective 3

Explain how insurance derivatives operate, including:

- **The use of swaps**
- **The use of insurance options**
- **The advantages and disadvantages of insurance derivatives**

Key Words and Phrases

Insurance derivative

Insurance option

Review Questions

3-1. Describe how an insurer might use a swap to spread its risk.

3-2. Describe an insurance option holder's potential gain in these situations:

   a. When the value of an underlying asset exceeds the strike price

   b. When the value of an underlying asset is below the strike price

3-3. List the advantages associated with insurance derivatives.

3-4. List the disadvantages associated with insurance derivatives.

Application Question

3-5. How might a theme park use an insurance option to level its income in a season having numerous rainy weekends?

Educational Objective 4

Explain how these contingent capital arrangements operate:

- **The use of a standby credit facility**
- **The use of a contingent surplus note arrangement**
- **The use of a catastrophe equity put arrangement**
- **The advantages and disadvantages of contingent capital arrangements**

Key Words and Phrases

Standby credit facility

Surplus note

Contingent surplus notes

Catastrophe equity put option

Review Questions

4-1. Identify the factors that influence the amount of a capital commitment fee.

4-2. Identify the three categories into which contingent capital agreements generally fall.

4-3. Identify the crucial difference between a standby credit facility and an insurance policy.

4-4. Identify the primary benefit associated with surplus notes.

4-5. Identify the advantages of contingent capital arrangements.

4-6. Identify the disadvantages of contingent capital arrangements.

Educational Objective 5

Analyze the concerns of organizations that use insurance-linked securities and insurance derivatives to transfer risk and the investors supplying capital.

Key Word or Phrase

Objective trigger

Review Questions

5-1. Identify the three elements about which organizations that use insurance-linked securities and insurance derivatives to transfer risk are concerned.

5-2. Identify why insurance-linked securities are considered to provide a high level of financial security.

5-3. Contrast structured options with traditional insurance.

5-4. Define objective trigger.

Educational Objective 6
Describe the regulatory and accounting issues involved with insurance-linked securities and insurance derivatives.

Review Questions

6-1. Identify the criteria used to determine whether an insurance securitization or insurance derivative can be considered insurance and regulated as such.

6-2. Describe the difference in regulatory and accounting treatment for insurance-linked securities and insurance derivatives that are determined to be insurance and those that are determined not to be insurance.

6-3. Explain how the use of a special purpose vehicle (SPV) provides an organization transferring its risk with tax and accounting advantages.

Answers to Assignment 10 Questions

NOTE: These answers are provided to give students a basic understanding of acceptable types of responses. They often are not the only valid answers and are not intended to provide an exhaustive response to the questions.

Educational Objective 1

1-1. With catastrophe bonds, a special purpose vehicle (SPV) "reinsures" the insurer for specific catastrophe losses and in turn funds the coverage by selling bonds in the regular capital markets. The interest and principal on these bonds does not need to be repaid to the capital market investors if the specified losses take place. If the losses do not take place, the SPV pays interest and repays the principal on a schedule, as with most other bonds.

1-2. An insurance derivative is a financial contract whose value is based on the level of insurable losses that occur during a specific time period. An insurance derivative increases in value as specified insurable losses increase, and, therefore, the purchaser of the derivative can use this gain to offset its insurable losses.

1-3. A contingent capital arrangement is a pre-loss agreement that establishes terms for an organization to raise cash in the wake of a major loss. The entity that agrees to provide the contingent capital receives a commitment fee in exchange for its promise to reimburse the partner organization for its loss costs. Under a contingent capital arrangement, the organization does not transfer its risk of loss to investors. Instead, after a loss occurs, it receives a capital injection in the form of debt or equity to help it pay for the loss. Because the terms of the capital injection are agreed upon in advance, the organization generally receives more favorable terms than it would receive if it were forced to raise capital after a large loss, when the organization is likely to be in a weakened financial condition.

Educational Objective 2

2-1. Instead of selling income-producing assets to a special purpose vehicle (SPV) and receiving cash—the process for most types of securitization—an organization engaging in an insurance securitization pays cash to the SPV, who sells insurance-linked securities (ILSs) to investors on the capital market. The SPV retains the principal from the security sales until the loss threshold specified in the ILS contract is met or the security expires. If the loss threshold is met, the SPV reimburses the organization for qualifying losses that occur up to the specified limit. At the end of the ILS period, the SPV may withhold from the investor the principal, the interest, or both, depending on the terms of the agreement; if the loss threshold is not met and the security expires, the SPV returns the principal to the investors along with interest earnings.

2-2. Catastrophe bonds are issued by special purpose vehicles developed and owned by large reinsurers, insurers, or large corporations to serve as catastrophe bond intermediaries and to mimic traditional excess (catastrophe) insurance (and reinsurance). The catastrophe losses that trigger payment under a catastrophe bond can be based on aggregate catastrophe losses over a defined period of time or the occurrence of a single catastrophic event. Losses triggered on an aggregate basis can be measured using an insurance industry loss index for catastrophes or using the actual catastrophe losses of an organization; they can also be measured against a specific standard (such as a Category Four or greater hurricane).

2-3. Insurers (and reinsurers) maintain capital that is only a fraction of the total policy limits they sell. With insurance securitization, the organization's secure resources equal the loss limits provided by its contract with the special purpose vehicles (SPV), and the SPV's obligations to pay losses to the organization and to pay interest and principal to investors are fully collateralized with the SPV's highly liquid investments. Consequently, the insurance securitization provides greater financial security than insurance or reinsurance.

2-4. Two disadvantages of insurance securitization might cause Valerie to advise Arkwright against purchasing an ILS. The purchase of an ILS would expose Arkwright to volatility. The relationship between the return demanded by securitization investors and premiums for insurance (and reinsurance) varies depending on the attractiveness of ILSs to investors when compared with their other investment opportunities and the state of the insurance underwriting cycle. In this case, ILSs would be less attractive to investors compared with the growth of earnings from the stock market because the soft underwriting cycle would result in low pricing and market demand for insurance-linked products.

Also in this scenario, Arkwright's opportunity cost would be high because of the collateralized assets held by the SPV using liquid assets, compared with the higher returns available from riskier investments.

Educational Objective 3

3-1. When an insurer uses a swap arrangement to spread or diversify its risk, the swap becomes an insurance derivative with the underlying asset a portfolio of a specified class of insured risks for an individual insurer. The insurer may be able to limit exposure to specific geographic catastrophes and enhance the diversification of its portfolio.

3-2. These answers describe an insurance option holder's potential gain in these situations:

a. When the value of an option's underlying asset exceeds the strike price, the buyer can exercise (sell) and realize a gain.

b. When the value of an option's underlying asset is less than the strike price, the buyer cannot realize a gain by exercising the option.

3-3. Advantages associated with insurance derivatives include these:

- Additional risk capacity
- Lower in cost than insurance-linked securities
- Transparent pricing
- Opportunities for investors to exit during its term
- Standardized contracts
- Efficient claims and contract settlement

3-4. Disadvantages associated with insurance derivatives include these:

- Underdeveloped markets

- Basis risk

- Credit risk

- Uncertain regulatory and accounting treatment

3-5. The theme park could purchase an insurance weather option that would pay out if a set number of weekends within its peak business months experience more than a specified number of inches of rain.

Educational Objective 4

4-1. The amount of the capital commitment fee is influenced by several factors, including likelihood of loss event, interest rates of alternative investments, and credit risk of the organization trying to arrange for the contingent capital.

4-2. A contingent capital agreement generally falls into one of these categories:

- Standby credit facility

- Contingent surplus note

- Catastrophe equity put option

4-3. The crucial difference between a standby credit facility and an insurance policy is that a standby credit facility obligates the organization to pay back, with interest, a loan it uses to cover losses. Losses paid by insurance, however, do not have to be repaid. Therefore, a standby credit facility entails loss retention, while insurance entails loss transfer.

4-4. The primary benefit associated with surplus notes is that they increase an insurer's assets without increasing its liabilities.

4-5. The advantages of contingent capital arrangements are these:

- The funds they make available to an organization cost less than funds made available by insurance.

- They allow an organization to obtain capital infusion at a predetermined price.

4-6. The disadvantages of contingent capital arrangements are these:

- Funds received from a standby credit facility or contingent surplus note for losses are paid in the form of loans, not equity, and must be paid back to the lender with interest.

- The amount of an organization's equity increases when a catastrophe equity put option is exercised, thereby reducing the existing shareholders' percentage of ownership. This dilution may also come at a crucial time in the management of the organization (that is, after a catastrophe).

Educational Objective 5

5-1.   The organizations that use insurance-linked securities and insurance derivatives to transfer risk are concerned with cost, the financial security (credit risk) of the parties supplying the risk capital, and the risk that the amount received may not match the amount of their loss (basis risk).

5-2.   Insurance-linked securities are considered to provide a high level of financial security because they are usually fully collateralized.

5-3.   Structured options, like traditional insurance, are usually tailored to the organization. However, structured options have slightly higher basis risk than traditional insurance, as options normally settle to an index or are based on an agreed value, rather than providing indemnification for actual losses.

5-4.   An objective trigger is a measurement that determines the value of an insurance-related capital market product based on a parameter that is not within the control of the organization transferring the risk.

Educational Objective 6

6-1.   These criteria are used to determine whether an insurance securitization or insurance derivative can be considered insurance and regulated as insurance:

- The contract must indemnify an organization for its actual losses.

- The insured organization must have an insurable interest that is the subject of an insurance contract.

Insurance securitizations and insurance derivatives whose values are based on an objective trigger may not be considered insurance and should not be regulated as insurance.

6-2.   Regulatory and accounting treatment for insurance-linked securities (ILSs) and insurance derivatives that are determined to be insurance must comply with insurance regulations. State premium taxes need to be paid; however, an organization can deduct these taxes and is not required to record outstanding losses that are covered by the insurance on the liability section of the balance sheet.

Investors in insurance-linked securities and insurance derivatives that are not determined to be insurance must comply with the requirements of the various regulators of securities and derivatives. An organization is not able to deduct for tax purposes the amount it pays to transfer risk, and it must record on its balance sheet outstanding losses that are meant to be covered by proceeds from the insurance-linked security or insurance derivative. The organization can show a corresponding asset on its balance sheet for the fair value of the insurance-linked security or insurance derivative.

6-3.   An organization transferring its risk of loss through an SPV receives tax and accounting advantages because the transaction will be treated as insurance or reinsurance if the SPV qualifies as an insurer or a reinsurer under U.S. state regulations.

Direct Your Learning

11

Allocating Costs of Managing Hazard Risk

Educational Objectives

After learning the content of this assignment, you should be able to:

1. Describe the purposes of allocating hazard risk management costs.

2. Describe the types of hazard risk management costs an organization may want to allocate.

3. Describe the prospective and retrospective approaches to allocating hazard risk management costs.

4. Describe the exposure bases and experience bases used to allocate hazard risk management costs.

5. Describe the practical considerations when selecting a hazard risk management cost allocation basis.

6. Given a case, justify how hazard risk management costs may be allocated among an organization's departments.

Outline

▶ **Purpose of Allocating Hazard Risk Management Costs**

A. Promote Risk Control

B. Facilitate Risk Retention

C. Prioritize Risk Management Expenditures

D. Reduce Costs

E. Distribute Costs Fairly

1. Balance Risk Bearing and Risk Sharing

2. Provide Managers With Risk Management Cost Information

3. Internal Manipulation

4. External Manipulation

▶ **Types of Hazard Risk Management Costs to Be Allocated**

A. Costs of Accidental Losses Not Reimbursed by Insurance or Other Outside Sources

1. Allocated and Unallocated Loss Adjustment Expenses

2. Allocating Retained Losses

3. Risk Charges

B. Insurance Premiums

C. Costs of Risk Control Techniques

D. Costs of Administering Risk Management Activities

▶ **Prospective and Retrospective Cost Allocation**

A. Prospective Cost Allocation Approach

B. Retrospective Cost Allocation Approach

▶ **Bases for Allocating Hazard Risk Management Costs**

A. Allocating Hazard Costs

B. Exposure Bases

1. General Liability

2. Automobile Liability

3. Workers Compensation

4. Property

5. Other Exposures

C. Experience Basis

1. Per Occurrence Limit

2. Aggregate Limit

3. Experience Period

▶ **Risk Management Cost Allocation—Practical Considerations**

▶ **Allocating Costs for Hazard Risk Management**

A. Case Facts

B. Case Analysis Steps

1. Determining an Effective Hazard Cost Allocation System

2. Identifying the Costs to Be Allocated

3. Choosing Between Prospective and Retrospective Allocations

4. Determining the Value and Method for Allocating Costs

5. Identifying Challenges and Opportunities

6. Performing Trial Calculations

If you are not sure that you have the current materials for the exam you plan to take, please contact The Institutes.

For each assignment, you should define or describe each of the Key Words and Phrases and answer each of the Review and Application Questions.

Educational Objective 1
Describe the purposes of allocating hazard risk management costs.

Key Words and Phrases

Risk-bearing system

Risk-sharing system

Review Questions

1-1.   Identify the costs of risk on which a hazard risk management cost allocation system should focus.

1-2.   Describe the purposes of an effective hazard risk management cost allocation system.

1-3. Describe how an organization can avoid internal and external manipulation of cost information provided by a hazard risk management cost allocation system.

Application Question

1-4. Foreway Corporation's Marketing Department has two divisions, one for its inside sales staff and one for its outside sales staff, which calls on customers in person. Each division has its own manager. The manager of the inside sales staff objects to the organization's allocation of the workers compensation premium, which is currently split evenly among the two divisions. Foreway has 40 percent more employees involved in inside sales than in outside sales. However, the outside sales staff experiences workers compensation losses that are ten times as frequent and severe as the inside staff's. Despite this, the manager of the outside sales division believes more of the workers compensation premium should be allocated to the inside sales division because it employs more workers and consumes more payroll. How should Foreway's risk management professional resolve this dispute?

Educational Objective 2

Describe the types of hazard risk management costs an organization may want to allocate.

Review Questions

2-1. List four types of hazard risk management costs that can be fully or partially allocated that constitute an organization's cost of risk.

2-2. Identify the costs that are most appropriately allocated to a particular department within a company.

2-3. Describe the bases upon which an organization calculates loss costs.

2-4. Identify the costs associated with administering risk management activities.

Application Question

2-5. Galston's risk management professional believes her estimation of the organization's future retained losses may differ substantially from the actual losses it will incur over the next accounting period. If her estimate is too high, any excess funds allocated to and charged to a department can be returned. However, if her estimate is too low, Galston's financial health could be jeopardized if it does not have the resources it needs to pay the higher-than-expected retained losses. What can she do to prepare Galston for potential adverse fluctuations in its retained losses, and how should it account for the solution on its financial statements?

Educational Objective 3
Describe the prospective and retrospective approaches to allocating hazard risk management costs.

Review Questions

3-1. Describe these widely used approaches to hazard risk management cost allocation:

a. Prospective cost allocation

b. Retrospective cost allocation

3-2. Describe the budgeting advantages of each of these approaches to hazard risk management cost allocation:

    a.   Prospective cost allocation

    b.   Retrospective cost allocation

3-3. Describe how the ease of evaluating hazard risk control program effectiveness differs depending on the cost allocation approach used.

Application Question

3-4. XYZ Corporation's loss history has consistently been better than the industry average for the last five years. Management feels the hazard risk control efforts of its departmental managers have, with few exceptions, been adequate. Senior management knows the corporation's board of directors believes that stable budgets indicate competent management. As the risk management professional for XYZ, would you recommend a prospective or retrospective cost allocation approach, and why?

Educational Objective 4

Describe the exposure bases and experience bases used to allocate hazard risk management costs.

Key Words and Phrases

Exposure-based system

Experience-based system

Experience period

Review Questions

4-1. List characteristics used to measure a loss exposure for hazard cost allocation purposes.

4-2. Identify commonly used bases for measuring and allocating costs for these loss exposures:

a. General liability

b.   Automobile liability

c.   Workers compensation

d.   Property

4-3. Identify methods an organization might use to allocate hazard risk management overhead.

4-4. List three primary criteria used to project a department's future losses and related costs.

Application Question

4-5. XYZ Corporation's risk management professional has learned the production department is about to launch a new product line. Several of the new products are being rushed to market because of intense competition and were not as thoroughly tested for safety as the risk management professional would have preferred. The corporation uses a prospective experience basis to allocate hazard risk management costs. Explain what experience period the production department managers will likely request and, if granted, what tools the risk management professional can use to make the allocation equitable among the corporation's other departments in light of the high potential for future product liability claims.

Educational Objective 5
Describe the practical considerations when selecting a hazard risk management cost allocation basis.

Review Questions

5-1. List issues relevant to an organization that is selecting a hazard risk management cost allocation basis.

5-2. Explain why some organizations may charge each department a minimum amount or maximum amount for risk management services.

5-3. Identify situations that typically trigger cost allocation system changes.

Application Question

5-4. Zelles is an international conglomerate with subsidiaries in several different countries. The management of each foreign subsidiary has been granted the authority to purchase its own insurance rather than participate in a centralized risk management cost allocation system. What problems may this create for a risk management professional responsible for appropriate cost allocation for the entire conglomerate?

Educational Objective 6

Given a case, justify how hazard risk management costs may be allocated among an organization's departments.

Application Questions

6-1. Toque Enterprises' risk management professional, Tyler, developed a retrospective hazard risk management cost allocation system for the organization, based on its four business departments. The organization is housed in a single building, so each department is subject to similar property loss exposures. Management wishes to reward departments based on their respective risk control efforts. Currently, the only measure of risk control costs is Toque's property, liability, and workers compensation insurance premiums, which total $240,000 per year. The Marketing Department incurred the greatest number of total property, liability, and workers compensation losses for the year at 40 percent, while each of the other departments incurred 20 percent of the losses.

Explain and calculate the Marketing Department's hazard risk management cost allocation for the coming year.

6-2. Dunsing Corporation's risk management professional, Sally, is charged with developing a plan to allocate the organization's hazard risk management costs among its three business units located within the city:

(1) The Garden Avenue (GA) unit has 5,000 square feet and earned 50 percent of the organization's annual revenue in the past year.

(2) The Plaza West (PW) unit has 7,000 square feet and earned 20 percent of the organization's annual revenue in the past year.

(3) The Urban Range (UR) unit has 4,000 square feet and earned 30 percent of the organization's revenue in the past year.

The UR unit is in a rough area of the city and is subject to high incidence of vandalism and malicious mischief losses. As a result, hazard losses for the UR unit are 60 percent of the organization's total losses over the past four years, and the remaining losses are equally distributed between the other two units. Sally believes that the UR unit could improve its loss experience considerably by successfully implementing some procedural changes and security measures. Over the past four years, the only hazard risk management cost to be allocated is the Dunsing's property-liability insurance cost.

Dunsing's CEO supports a hazard cost allocation system that rewards business units based on their revenue contribution for the past year equally with their successful hazard risk management efforts over the past four years. Because of the disadvantage of the UR unit's location, the CEO has provided a small budget for hazard risk management measures and discretion for its management to determine the best use of the funds. Sally will take a retrospective approach to hazard risk management cost allocation, so the UR unit's risk management success will affect its cost allocation for the following year, when results are recognized.

a. Suggest a retrospective hazard risk management allocation system that Sally could implement that would encourage profits and hazard risk management for Dunsing's business units.

b. Determine the hazard risk management cost allocation for Dunsing's UR unit based on the percentages given and Sally's cost allocation system.

c. Explain in what way the cost allocation system will be affected by the UR unit's hazard risk management budget in the following year.

6-3. Acre Manufacturing Company's risk management professional wishes to allocate the organization's upcoming $180,000 annual products liability premium among Departments A, B, and C, the departments that produce the organization's three products. The allocations are to be based one-third on each department's sales for the past year and two-thirds on the products liability claims paid for each department's products over the past three years, with the portion of each claim charged to each department capped at $25,000. The relevant sales and capped paid claim dollar amounts are as shown in the table

By entering the missing values in the table below, calculate each department's premium allocation for products liability insurance for the coming year.

Department	1 Sales (millions)	2 Percentage of total sales: Sales per department Total	3 Losses (thousands)	4 Percentage of total losses: Losses per department Total	5 Weighted percentage (1/3 sales and 2/3 losses): [Col. 2 + (2 × Col. 4)] / 3	6 Allocation per department of the $180,000 products liability premium: $\left(\dfrac{\text{Col. 5}}{100}\right) \times \$180{,}000$
A	80		30			
B	40		20			
C	20		60			
Total	$140	100	$110	100	100	$180,000

Answers to Assignment 11 Questions

NOTE: These answers are provided to give students a basic understanding of acceptable types of responses. They often are not the only valid answers and are not intended to provide an exhaustive response to the questions.

Educational Objective 1

1-1. An effectively designed hazard risk management cost allocation system should focus on these costs of risk:

- Retained losses

- Insurance premiums

- Risk control costs

- Administrative expenses for the risk management function

1-2. An effective cost allocation system serves these purposes:

- Promote risk control—Motivates personnel to reduce the frequency and/or severity of the organization's losses because each department is held accountable or rewarded for its risk control efforts.

- Facilitate risk retention—Allows the entire organization to benefit from an optimal risk retention level while not unduly exposing individual departments to excessive fluctuations in their cost of risk.

- Prioritize risk management expenditures—Departments that pay for risk control measures carefully scrutinize the measure's cost effectiveness and prioritize measures that provide the greatest return on investment.

- Reduce costs—Lowering claim frequency and severity through risk control allows an organization to retain risk at an optimal level, resulting in a lower cost of risk.

- Distribute costs fairly—Assigned amounts should have a direct correlation between departmental losses and the amount of risk management costs allocated to the unit.

- Balance risk bearing and risk sharing—A proper balance distributes risk management costs across the organization while also allowing departments to benefit from their own loss experience and other changing conditions.

- Provide managers with hazard risk management cost information—Accurate allocation and reporting of cost of risk compels managers to focus on areas in which the cost of risk can be reduced.

1-3. Internal and external manipulation of cost information can be avoided in these ways:

- Internal manipulation of cost information can be discouraged or prevented by requiring losses to be reviewed or audited to confirm that they were reported in a timely fashion and that subsequent changes to reserve amounts are not attributable to facts that should have been revealed at the time of the loss.

- External manipulation may be prevented if the system is designed to reflect the organization's overall objectives and has been approved by senior management.

1-4. An effective hazard cost allocation system addresses the concerns of both division managers. The inside sales division appears to have more exposure at first glance because of its higher number of employees and its larger payroll. However, the outside sales division has far more frequent and severe claims than the inside sales division. Some risk management professionals would argue that this is because outside sales jobs are much riskier. Consequently, the outside sales division's overall workers compensation loss exposure is higher than the inside sales division's. Therefore, the most equitable solution is to increase the outside sales division's premium allocation. The manager of the inside sales division should be satisfied with the decreased premium allocation. The manager of the outside sales division should focus on preventing or reducing the frequency and severity of the division's losses.

Educational Objective 2

2-1. These are four types of hazard risk management costs that constitute an organization's cost of risk:

- Costs of accidental losses not reimbursed by insurance or other outside sources

- Insurance premiums

- Costs of risk control techniques

- Costs of administering risk management activities

2-2. Costs most appropriately allocated to a department include those that are clearly incurred by and beneficial to the department and that are wholly within its control.

2-3. An organization calculates loss costs on one of these bases:

- Incurred loss basis—Amounts paid for losses are added to reserves for pending claims, to the additions to those reserves, and to the estimated amount of incurred but not reported losses.

- Claims-made basis—Actual loss payments are added to changes in reserves for claims made during the accounting period.

- Claims-paid basis—Amount paid on losses during the accounting period, regardless of when the losses were incurred.

2-4. These costs are associated with administering risk management activities:

- Operating budget of the risk management department

- Cost of executives' time from other departments

- Other resources from other departments devoted to hazard risk management

2-5. The risk management professional should consider adding a risk charge when calculating retained losses that are to be allocated. The risk charge is an amount added to an organization's expected losses to cover potential adverse fluctuation in experience. The risk charge is not a liability and should not be shown as such on Galston's financial statements. It should be shown as a segregated part of Galston's equity.

Educational Objective 3

3-1. These are the two general approaches to hazard risk management cost allocation:

a. Estimated costs are allocated at the beginning of the accounting period during which they are expected to be incurred. But once allocated, costs are not changed for the period, regardless of actual losses incurred.

b. Estimated costs are allocated at the beginning of the accounting period during which they are expected to be incurred, but they can be reallocated one or more times during or after the close of the period, with payments or returns made retrospectively according to changes in loss experience.

3-2. These are the advantages of each hazard risk management cost allocation approach:

a. Costs are assumed to be known before the beginning of the accounting period and are not changed.

b. Costs are more accurately attributed to the period and department with which they are associated. However, final allocated costs are not determined until well after the end of the period during which the losses were incurred, which complicates risk management budgeting.

3-3. The ease of evaluating the effectiveness of a risk control program differs in these ways, depending on the cost allocation approach selected:

- Prospective cost allocation—An increase (or decrease) in risk control activity can be separated by several accounting periods from the corresponding reduction (or increase) in allocated costs and are not always reflective of risk control expense outputs of the period to which they are charged.

- Retrospective cost allocation—Hazard risk control program effectiveness is facilitated because the decrease (or increase) in loss costs is immediately recognized in terms of allocated costs.

3-4. XYZ should adopt a prospective cost allocation approach because such an approach typically produces a more stable budget, which is important to the board of directors. XYZ's losses have also been stable and below the industry average, which indicates its departmental managers are practicing appropriate risk control. This also suggests that prospective cost allocation would be the best approach.

Educational Objective 4

4-1. Characteristics used to measure a loss exposure for hazard cost allocation purposes include size, nature of operations, and territory.

4-2. These answers identify commonly used bases for measuring and allocating costs for these corresponding loss exposures:

a. Commonly used bases for general liability include square footage of floor space, annual budget, payroll, full-time-equivalent workers, and sales.

b. The commonly used basis for automobile liability is the number of vehicles used, with some adjustments for differences in types of vehicles.

c. Commonly used bases for workers compensation include payroll and full-time equivalent number of employees, with adjustments made for differences in exposure by job classification.

d. Commonly used bases for property include square footage and property values (either replacement cost or actual cash value). The exposure base is often modified to accurately reflect the associated exposure.

4-3. An organization may use these methods to allocate hazard risk management overhead:

- In proportion to the total of other risk management department costs allocated for particular loss exposures

- As a fixed percentage of some other basis, such as sales

- As a combination of a flat fee per department (to cover fixed costs) and a percentage of some base, such as sales (to cover variable costs)

4-4. These three primary criteria are used to project a department's losses and related costs:

- Changes in claims paid

- Changes in payments plus loss reserves

- Changes in projected ultimate incurred losses

4-5. XYZ's production department managers are likely to favor an extended reporting period (for example, a full five years). A longer experience period should make the cost allocation formula less responsive to changes in recent past loss experience, which limits the fluctuation of charges that results from unusually bad claim experience. In response, the risk management professional can weight the multiyear experience period to more heavily count recent experience. For example, if the production managers are granted a five-year experience period, the most recent year can be weighted by 20 percent, the second and third years weighted by 15 percent each, and the fourth and fifth years weighted by 10 percent each.

Educational Objective 5

5-1. Issues relevant to an organization that is selecting a hazard risk management cost allocation basis include these:

- Accounting system
- Tax system
- Minimum amount charge for each department
- Whether cost allocation is significant
- Penalties or rewards for department managers
- Inclusion of managers in development of the risk management cost allocation plan
- The risk management information systems (RMIS) used
- Consistency of cost allocation
- Changes in organizational structure

5-2. Some organizations may charge each department a minimum amount for risk management services to incorporate an exposure basis within the hazard risk management cost allocation system. A maximum amount might be charged to reduce the fluctuations in allocated costs from one accounting period to the next.

5-3. These situations typically trigger cost allocation system changes:

- Material shifts in the organization's operations
- Change in expected losses because of change in legal climate, inflation, or some other factor, which can create a need to change the per occurrence limit
- Restructuring of the organization's departments or lines of authority

5-4. When each subsidiary of Zelles purchases its own insurance, the combined purchasing power of the organization is not leveraged. This limits the subsidiaries' ability to negotiate lower expense factors and service fees from an insurer. Also, gaps in coverage or duplications of coverage may result. In addition, consistent application of umbrella or excess liability insurance policies presents a challenge.

Educational Objective 6

6-1. Because the only measure of risk control costs is the organization's $240,000 total insurance premium and the Marketing Department incurred 40 percent of the losses, 40 percent of the insurance premium cost would be allocated to that department. This would be calculated as $240,000 × 0.40 = $96,000.

6-2.   These answers are based on the Dunsing Corporation case.

    a.   To allocate hazard risk management costs among Dunsing's three business units in a way that would reward profits, Sally should include each unit's revenue percentage in the cost allocation. To reward successful risk management efforts, Sally should include each unit's loss percentage over the four-year period in the allocation. She should weight the revenue percentage equally with the loss experience percentage by adding the two percentages for each unit together and dividing by two (50 percent for revenue allocation and 50 percent for loss allocation). The result will be an appropriate hazard risk management allocation.

    b.   The UR unit earns 30 percent of the profits of the organization and incurs 60 percent of the losses. Together these percentages total 90 percent. That percentage divided by two is 45 percent for the current year.

    c.   The UR unit's hazard risk management expenditure should be added to Dunsing's insurance premium for the following year to develop the loss experience percentages for that year. Because the budget amount was intended to help equalize the UR unit's results, the amount spent from that budget should be allocated equally among the three units before applying the loss experience percentages.

6-3.   The allocations for Departments A, B, and C (the values in Column 6) are calculated as shown in the answer exhibit.

Department	1 Sales (millions) Sales per department / Total	2 Percentage of total sales:	3 Losses (thousands)	4 Percentage of total losses: Losses per department / Total	5 Weighted percentage (1/3 sales and 2/3 losses): $\frac{[\text{Col. 2} + (2 \times \text{Col. 4})]}{3}$	6 Allocation per department of the $180,000 products liability premium: $\left(\frac{\text{Col. 5}}{100}\right) \times \$180{,}000$
A	80	57	30	27	37	66,600
B	40	29	20	18	22	39,600
C	20	14	60	55	41	73,800
Total	$140	100	$110	100	100	$180,000